Teatre-Museu Dalí

J. L. Giménez-Frontín

Teatre-Museu Dalí

Fundació Gala-Salvador Dalí

Tusquets/Electa

Translation
Anthony John Keily

Phototypesetting
Safekat, S. L.

Color Separation
Lucam, S. A.

Printing and Binding
Jomagar

Index

Foreword

This guide is intended merely to accompany the visitor around the labyrinthine spaces of the Teatre-Museu Dalí (Figueres) with a few —and I hope at least minimally enlightening— comments on its most significant pieces.

I feel it my duty to point out, however, that the text of this guide is a shorter adaptation of the guide-catalogue which offers the reader a more detailed visit to the Teatre Museu.

All the same, too many interpretative hypotheses, some of which will appear questionable or less than essential, have undoubtedly slipped into the following pages, but perhaps these will stimulate the interest or creative imagination of some readers. Indeed, Dalí's work —each piece exhibited and indeed the Teatre-Museu itself— is an *open work*, susceptible to multiple readings and interpretations, perhaps comparable to an endless set of Russian dolls. I mean by this that any critical reading of Dalí's work is bound always to partial clarification, since it is unlikely to exhaust the full range of resonances contained in that work. My reading, obviously limited by the large number of pieces to be treated, as well as by the nature of this guide, is even less likely than most to exhaust its range. In any case, given the informative aim of the guide, I have decided against any kind of studious approach, and resisted the temptation to turn the visit into a *collage* of quotes and footnotes. Besides, it seems that I am thus remaining more faithful to the wishes of Salvador Dalí who, as is well known, was against having his Teatre-Museu turned into a rigid "catalogue" in the usual sense, which would dilute the Dalinian spirit.

Finally, it is obvious that this approach to the memory and work of Dalí would not have been possible without reference to many Dalinian specialists, among whom I feel I should mention R. Descharnes, I. Gómez de Liaño, C. Rodríguez Aguilera, L. Romero, P. Roumeguère and R. Santos Torroella, as well as R. Guardiola Rovira, chronicler of the administration of the museum. The museum-related information was very kindly made available to me by the efficient team at the Gala-Salvador Dalí Foundation, made up of M. Aguer, J. Artigas, P. Aldámiz, G. Berini, J. M. Guillamet and M. T. Brugués. Very special thanks to Félix Fanés and Montserrat Aguer, Director and Coordinator, respectively, of the Dalí Study Centre at the Gala-Salvador Dalí Foundation, for their wise observations and suggestions, and also to Pilar Daniel for her careful reading of the final text. My main acknowledgement must however go to the painter Antoni Pitxot, Director of the Teatre-Museu, whose limitless memory has been the cornerstone for the reconstruction of Dalí's wishes in the execution of a number of works and their location throughout the spaces we visit in the following pages.

Finally, if, apart from serving its primary function, this guide contributes to the undoing of some of the most stubborn commonplaces adhering to the fascinating and controversial creative genius of Salvador Dalí, then it will more than have fulfilled its aims.

J. L. Giménez-Frontín
Cadaqués, August 1993

Teatre-Museu Dalí, the incarnation and commemoration of Dalí and his work

The Teatre-Museu, or Theatre-Museum, in Figueres is not merely a *museum* even if it does contain some of the most important and significant works produced by Dalí (or indeed in the history of surrealist art). In itself —container and content— it is a Dalinian piece, a work to which Salvador Dalí, with his typical stubbornness and thoroughness, devoted thirteen years of his life. Susceptible to all sorts of incorporations and transformations, it is an experience which aims to do away with the passivity of spectators who suddenly find themselves in the role of accomplices; it is therefore also a truly surrealist experience.

To understand what Salvador Dalí intended with this museum that he dedicated to his native town of Figueres will be to understand the very keys to the Dalinian method, which, despite appearances, have little or nothing gratuitous or absurd in them.

First and foremost it should be remembered that in his work Dalí never allows himself to be drawn deliriously by his imagination; he rather sets about mastering it methodically, even coldly, in order to attain previously established goals: to make use of the external world as an irrefutable illustration and proof of another —obsessive— reality, which is that of our spirit; what is involved is thus not the "illustration" of dream passages or fantasies induced by a state of trance or automatic delirium, but rather on the contrary the provocation of the experience of a virtual reality produced by associations which are at once delirious and rigorously logical. This method, defined by Dalí as "paranoiac-critical", went on to revolutionize the ranks of Parisian surrealism in 1929 and did away with the innocent techniques of "automatic" writing and painting.

Let us thus keep in mind when we enter the spaces of the Teatre-Museu that the pieces on display —but also the very arrangement and structure of the museum in so far as it is a creation of Dalí— are the product of the logic of an obsessive and meticulous mind. To this end even the blooming of chance can be channelled and harmoniously integrated inside a pre-conceived and extremely coherent plan. Which in turn requires us to go into the main outlines and master keys of the Dalinian universe.

The reader who has already visited the Teatre-Museu might well asked what key or keys can be provided by the work of an extremely fertile and many-sided creator who, from his earliest childhood paintings in the impressionist mould, expressed himself in a variety of aesthetic registers, and who, to make matters worse, decided to offer his work to the public in a chronological mess, even going so far as to display his pieces untitled and undated.

It is obvious that Dalí imposes a reading of his universe from an exclusive and excluding perspective which allows it to form a coherent and unitary whole. Things may not turn out so simply, however, for the critic or art historian. Thus what could be termed his period of searching and apprenticeship stretches from his first "catalogued" work, painted when he was only ten, up to when he was about twenty; throughout

Dalí with Gala, giving instructions for the alterations and building of the Teatre-Museu. Left and seated by the Rainy Cadillac, Antoni Pitxot.

this period, first the child prodigy, and then the young hopeful, would practise, master and abandon in succession the techniques and aesthetic principles of impressionism, pointillism, Catalan *noucentisme*, neo-cubism, and even those of the poetic cosmology of Joan Miró. We are not dealing here with mere exercises. The young Dalí's talent is amazing, and his work is unmistakable from the "Freudian" phase on, which culminated in the violent and emblematic works produced in 1927. These involve an evolutionary process which cannot really be separated from his later subscription to Parisian surrealism and the formulation of the "paranoiac-critical" method in 1929.

From 1941 to the end of his days Salvador Dalí would combine his extremely personal paranoiac-critical creativity with the defence of a basically neo-classical realism, an explosive combination which allowed him to indulge in all kinds of visual experiments (or phenomenological reflections) in order to manifest his "scientific" obsessions (the product of a unusually high degree of curiosity and knowledge). In short, what he was doing was materialising his very peculiar version of a mysticism which I would go so far as to term materialist, which was first given written form in 1951. A tragic mysticism.

Regardless of the successive aesthetic tendencies, however, of Salvador Dalí's work, from a thematic point of view it is always autobiographical, even exhibitionist. But also autobiographical in an internal sense, as a faithful reflection of his spiritual crises, terrors, obsessions, of his "spiritual" visions and obsessions.

This "autobiography" is, let it be said, written in an iconography of symbols, which together make up a closed universe of "extra-artistic" referents. In order to understand the scope of this central point, allow me to engage in one previous reflection.

Especially from 1927 on, Salvador Dalí erects his work as a monument against the artistic criteria of modernity, according to which art should only have its own specific language as its object and referent. For Dalí, this process necessarily led to negativity and a complete vacuum. Artistic languages should be mastered, according to Dalí, as a necessary starting point and not as the sole objective of creation. The referents are pre-existing and external because they express a reading (and an objective reading) of the reality of the world. In this sense it is right to term the Dalinian creative whole as *narrative*, regardless of the specific aesthetic with which he formulated it. And regardless also of the fact that he manifested it in literary and pictorial works, in sculpture and essays, or in all kinds of provocative performances.

The reality of the world for Salvador Dalí is, let it be stated, not the common and apparent reality, since what he aims at, first of all, is the artistic formulation of the main components of the unconscious ("virtual ghosts... with all of the attributes of realism proper to tangible objects"), and, secondly, the mastering of reality and consciousness by transmitting to us his phenomenological reflections and his scientific and mystical insights on the matter (mineral, carnal and "angelical") of the universe. We must therefore insist on the fact that Dalí does no more than propose readings on the "objective" laws regulating the life of the material, either in the sphere of the unconscious or in that of visions or intuitions of the essence of external reality (hidden under the most deceptive of appearances). This materialism is neither amiable nor sensual, but rather almost always violent and tragic. It has at its root an obsessive terror of the processes of material decomposition, of final death, and — in a parallel fashion — of the experience of sex, understood as the heralding of destruction and death. There is not the slightest trace of sentimentalism nor romanticism in the Dalinian universe (the glorification of Gala is not *sentimental*), as is proper in an analysis of matter (even "spiritualised" matter) as the exclusive principle of the mystery of life.

Dalí's relation to the reality of the world is, therefore, always rooted in and the exclusive product of his five senses; but these senses are governed, in his case, by a cold and rigorous intellectual process. This hypersensitivity is, in its turn the direct cause of some of the most obvious constants in the Dalinian creed: his conception of beauty as an "edible" and nutritious matter; his faithfulness to a particular external context (Dalí's *homeland* is not historical, abstract, but rather experiential, the "ultra-local" homeland of childhood, which according to the paradox of Montaigne, points us towards "universality"); his rejection of all subjective expressive aesthetics, in which not the object, but rather its resonance in the soul of the artist, is what is important; finally, his even stronger condemnation of art which, in terms of execution, turns its back on the reality of the senses, a type of art which, to make matters worse, was twinned according to him with a lack of technical skills (thus his declaration of war on the conceptual principles of informalism and his parallel exaltation of the renaissance masters, along with a provocative defence of the *pompier* painters of the nineteenth century).

In conclusion, from a strictly aesthetic point of view Dalí's work seems abstruse and incomprehensible if it is not viewed, from the earliest paintings on, as an incarnation of a unique meeting or a brilliant synthesis of classicism with the avant-garde, whose contradictory elements (both aesthetic and programmatic) are controlled by Salvador Dalí in the exclusive interest of his own work. Some of its most typical features belong, indeed, to a classicist tradition: basically the signifying ("narrative" or anti-modern) intention of Dalí's work. On the other hand other features such as his fanatical proselytism, and above all his provocative and nihilistic humour, are clearly "modern". (His provocative stance and humour have, incidentally, served as a shield to protect the more fragile aspects of his personality and have acted as a smoke-screen blocking out the most profound theses of Dalinian thought.) Still other features are of mixed origin. I refer

here to his ethical positions within the "revolutionary" orthodoxy of surrealism and, subsequently, his defence of the ethical and aesthetic standards of renaissance principles. It is
right to think, therefore, that the coherent nature of Dalinian
universe justifies the unusual arrangement of the spaces of
the Teatre-Museu in Figueres according to the wishes of
their author; these spaces surprisingly concede as much
importance to minor pieces as to masterpieces (from the
Dalinian, not art critic's, point of view). So Dalí worked not
for months but for years on his Teatre-Museu, as an element
of the Dalinian universe that would have to englobe all
others, his desires finally overcoming any reservations and
difficulties that arose.

Ramón Guardiola Rovira, a lawyer, was named mayor of
Figueres in 1960. He asked Dalí to donate a picture to the
Museo del Ampurdan in Figueres. His aim was not so much
to add to the wealth of the city as to render a homage to the
"son of Dalí, the notary", since Figueres, his native city,
had until then shown no "public sympathy for its illustrious
son."

Let us recall that Dalí was born in his family home, the former No. 20, Calle Narcís Monturiol in Figueres, on 11 May,
1904. Salvador, his father, a native of Cadaqués, was the
city's notary, and his mother, Felipa Doménech, was from
Barcelona. Dalí spent his schooldays in Figueres until he
entered the Academia de Bellas Artes de San Fernando and
the famous Residencia de Estudiantes in Madrid in September, 1922, where he would begin a close friendship with Federico García Lorca and Luis Buñuel. Years before, in 1918,
when he was just fourteen, he had held his first collective
exhibition in the vestibule of the Teatro Principal (the present Teatre-Museu). A local journalist chronicled the event
under the headline *Three Local Amateurs* and predicted that
"He will be a great painter."

Dalí's mother died in Figueres in 1921, a dramatic incident
for him; the young iconoclast, incidentally, only ever spoke
of her with affection and respect in his autobiographical writ-
ings. He returned to Figueres in 1923 after his temporary
expulsion from Bellas Artes and was arrested in the city in
May of 1924 (and spent a month in prison in Girona), because
of his revolutionary ideas. He did his military service in the
military castle in Figueres in 1927. It was in Figueres in
1929 that the young genius suffered the traumatic break
with his father and his sister Ana Maria, who were opposed
to the course his life and career were taking, and more specifically to his relationship with Gala Eluard (Gala, a "Russian" and an open adultress was, to make matters worse,
years older than the young Salvador). But Figueres was also
the setting for the family reconciliation in 1948, when Dalí
returned from the United States, not only "famous" — he
had been that for twenty years — but also financially com-
fortable.

It thus seems surprising that no cultural authority in
Figueres should have made any approach to this
"illustrious son" of the city until 1960. Indeed, neither was

any effort made at approaching him in the Catalan capital, Barcelona, where intellectual life was again coming to the boil after more than twenty years of cultural paralysis under Franco, while the cultural policies of the dictatorship did nothing to include him. The reasons for this are diverse, but today, with the wisdom of hindsight, it seems obvious that Dalinian provocation had irritated all of the cultural forces in the Spain of the time. The Franco regime's fascistic rhetoric and orthodox Catholicism mistrusted Dalí even when he declared himself to a Roman Catholic (sometimes a "Rumanian" Catholic). In the last analysis, his "realism" was not to be trusted either; it was a false realism, a troubling and in some shady way a deeply "subversive" realism. For the emerging culture of opposition to Franco, Dalí was that heterodox figure who had betrayed the principles of modernism, foretelling an inconceivable return to realism, besides being an artist without any political principles.

The main façade with scaffolding during the alterations and building of the Teatre-Museu.

Perhaps Dalí was secretly hurt by a situation that he only worsened with his public statements and really wanted to bring together his life and work in his native land. Indeed when in the autumn of 1960 he received a visit from his friend the photographer Melitón Casals, "Meli", bearing the request of the mayor of Figueres, his reply was immediate: he would donate a whole "museum" and not just a picture to Figueres. It was Dalí who declared that the museum should be set up in the gutted Teatro Principal in Figueres, the scene of his first collective exhibition. Dalí's project would have to wait for years however, until 1974, to become a reality.

The Teatro Principal was built in 1849 by the architect Roca Bros, the aim being to provide the city with a lyric auditorium in which companies visiting Barcelona's Liceo could perform. In 1939, when the outcome of the Civil War was already clear, Figueres witness the disorderly retreat of the Republican Army to France and suffered very severe bombardment from the "National" forces. The Teatro Principal, however, remained intact until Moroccan troops from Franco's army lit fires in its stalls to cook or stay warm and caused the fire that reduced it to ruins. From then on the theatre was no more than a dramatic semi-circular shell of blackened stone, open to the sky.

It should be noted that mayor Guardiola's reaction to Dalí's words was that of veritable statesman. He understood the importance of the project; he overcame the reservations and mistrust of his fellow citizens (who didn't want to be the butt of some Dalinian practical joke), got the noteworthy families of the Ampurdan region moving, and began to pull the complex strings of the administration and government under the dictatorship in search of funding. Finally, thirteen years later, on 28 September, 1974, the Teatre-Museu Dalí was opened. It contained, as the more optimistic had hoped, an important amount of the painter's own work (as well as pieces from his private collection). This was no ordinary museum, but rather, taken as a whole, a Dalinian creation on which the Port Lligat

Walls and arch of the stage of the Teatro Pirncipal before restoration.

painter had been working for more than a decade. It is worth highlighting a few key dates from this extended period of work.

Dalí stated to *Time* magazine in 1964 (paraphrasing the popular saying which describes anything destined to failure as a house built starting with the roof) that the first thing to be built in his museum would be the roof, in the form of a spectacular transparent latticed dome by Fuller to be fitted over the theatre's stage. In any case, it is symptomatic of Dalí's logic that in 1965, a full year after his comments in *Time*, with no clear financial commitment from Bellas Artes, Dalí not only presented his plans to the Barcelona press as a *fait accompli*, but insisted on the idea of the dome, adding what is more a new and spectacular element to the project: its positioning over the stage using a helicopter. (Today we know that this battle was finally won by Dalí's visionary imagination and that the latticed dome has come to be an emblem and identifying trait not only of the Teatre-Museu, but also of the city of Figueres.)

In 1968 he changed his strategy, deciding definitively against funding by Bellas Artes and initiating contacts with the Ministry of Tourism. Finally, two years later, on 26 June 1970, the Cabinet approved the project — under the auspices of the Ministry of Housing! The estimate for the work was approved by means of the application of a forgotten Decree in which the government had undertaken to make good some of the devastation caused by the Civil War (which had ended thirty years before!). Since Dalí was involved, even public administration seemed to be affected by surrealism. The estimate came to the modest sum of 12,212,168 pesetas, and the documents relating to the pro-

*Installation over the stage of the
latticed dome by Pérez Piñero.*

ject were signed by the architects Joaquín Ros de Ramis
and Alejandro Bonaterra.

Legal and economic reasons, however, prevented Fuller,
the US architect, from being the designer of the latticed
dome. Emilio Pérez Piñero, who had designed some similar projects, was proposed as an alternative and was
accepted enthusiastically by Dalí after a perusal of the
architect's work. Pérez Piñero would go on to become a
personal friend of Dalí's, as well as a creative interpreter
of his wishes, up until his death in a motor accident on 9
July 1972.

Work was begun on 13 October 1970. Exactly one month later
Dalí unveiled the central portion of the painting occupying
the main hall of the theatre (the present Palace of the Wind).
He would follow the ups and downs of the museum from then
on with meticulous enthusiasm.

The Teatre-Museu Dalí was finally offically opened on 28
October 1974 in the midst of a series of events which were
severely overcrowded by an avalanche of guests, journalists,
sympathizers and the merely curious. What was on show was
not a finished museum, but rather one in progress, open to
future incorporations of the artist's ideas and works; yet even

in 1974 it was a museum space which the writer Josep Pla termed "extraordinary".

A culmination of imagination and desire, and in itself a work of extreme Dalinian coherency outside any known canons of museum design, containing all sorts of creations that involved all sorts of materials and props, from childhood paintings to the last works executed in the castle of Púbol and the Torre Galatea, the Teatre-Museu deserves to be seen as a supreme demonstration of the triumph of desire over the obscene logic of reality.

It is equally a triumph of the persistence of memory, offered here to the coming generations. I am referring to the art of memory as a discipline involving knowledge and renovation, but also, more specifically, to the memory of Dalí's work. It is thus that the Port-Lligat painter (who was always partial to titles linked to the referents of his thought) gave the title or subtitle of the "Theatre of Memory" to his Teatre Museu.

It was to this theatre that he turned his last and perhaps melancholic gaze from his window in the Torre Galatea, already crushed by the death of Gala and by the annoyingly early arrival of his own death — a humiliation from which he was to be freed on 23 January, 1989. That morning, at a quarter past ten, Salvador Dalí "gave up his carnal spirit, in other words he died."

THE EXTERIOR OF THE MUSEUM. Even in the works located on the outside of the buildings, Dalí uncovers keys to the reading of his museum, taken in all as a Dalinian creation and not just a place to house collections. He also uses these works to present some of the most constant themes in his artistic universe, in which associations, groupings, appropriations, allusions, quotes and self-quotes are never gratuitous, but rather significant, integrating and cohering into a new reality which is the reality (both artistic and extra-artistic) of Dalinian creation. The first Dalinian feature we come to on the outside of the museum is precisely the radial design of the paving in the front area and the adjoining Plaza Gala-Salvador Dalí, whose radii converge towards the stage of the former theatre of Figueres, thus placed at the centre of Dalí's scenography. The first sculpture the visitor comes to at the entrance to the museum, set on a broad two-tiered pedestal, is a monument to the Catholic and Catalan writer Francesc Pujols (1882-1962), considered by Dalí as a master and precursor of structured thought by way of mental associations. This sculpture makes up a large *assemblage* of materials and meanings of different types which, taken as a whole and viewed from the front, can easily be visualised as a seated thinker, like Rodin's, dressed in the classical manner (wearing a ruff and cape) and with a golden hydrogen atom, an image of power and good government, to its right.

The bust of Pujols emerges from thick olive trunks; the olive tree is a benign emblem in Dalí's symbology. This nutritious tree is associated with the world of work (by way of its incorporation into the basse-relief montage *Trades and Crafts* by Guillot, executed for the Universal Exhibition in Paris in 1900), but also with the memory of the ultra-local "homeland of childhood", alluded to by way of this patrician individual who reminded Dalí of Pepito Pichot (the Pichots were a very important family in Dalí's childhood and in the awakening of his vocation as a painter). The golden head of the imposing seated thinker in turn reproduces the bulbous outline (related to the more intra-uterine outline of the egg) of the head of Narcissus, a recurrent symbol, from the 1936 painting and poem *The Metamorphosis of Narcissus* on, of rebirth and of flourishing. Lastly it is worth highlighting, at the rear of the assemblage, the figure of the theologian, mystic and alchemist Ramon Llull, of whom Pujols claimed to be a disciple, and whose presence is balanced, or perhaps fused, with the great golden hydrogen atom. The structure of the atom is an emblem of the perfection of nature (like the spiral of the snail shell, or the logarithmic cone of the rhinoceros's horn); but it also constitutes the image of a *continuum* of buttocks as a representation of the finite nature of the universe. The whole is also extremely significant as a declaration of anti-aesthetic, *kitsch*, prosaic and art laid principles, to which the painter would refer without qualms, whenever and however he saw fit, in the attainment of his goals.

The other large outdoor sculpture is located on the stairway leading from Carrer Jonquera to the Plaza Gala-Salvador Dalí. It is a large bronze entitled *Homage to Newton*, and clearly owes something to Pablo Gargallo and Henry Moore; a masculine figure with holes in its head and breast, it extends its arms sideways, dropping an apple theatrically from its right hand. The fall is frozen by the metal material of the sculpture, so that the falling apple is transformed into a rigid pendulum. (We will have the chance, in the *Palau del Vent*, or Palace of the Wind, to view one of the six pieces from the original edition, of smaller dimensions, of this statue.) There is an obviously destabilizing intention in the right foot of the sculpture, which looks as if it had been cut repeatedly and cruelly with an invisible hatchet and which is missing a few segments, although the toes are still in place; next to the foot we find an extra big toe, perhaps the product of an amputation suffered by some absent individual, or perhaps foreshadowing a future amputation affecting the figure itself.

In this same square we find three homages to Ernest Meissonier, a *pompier* painter very much praised by Dalí, partly to provoke, but also seriously for his ability to suggest "mystery". These are three reproductions in plaster and polyester of the monument to Meissonier by Antoni Mercié in 1895; these reproductions were elevated by Dalí to different levels by pedestals, made respectively of six, seven and seventeen tractor tyres, for his retrospective in the Georges Pompidou Centre in Paris in 1979 ($500 \times 200 \times 200$ cm approx. for the smaller montages, and $800 \times 200 \times 200$ cm approx. for the largest). They are indeed a donation to the Teatre-Museu from

Homage to Newton, *1985.*
Bronze sculpture, 38 × 200 × 134
cm, on the steps to Carrer de la
Jonquera.

Homage to Newton, *1985.*
Bronze 380 × 200 × 134 cm,
detail.

the Centre. It is worth highlighting Dalí's re-use of waste
material, of tyres that are piled high like black funeral alters
in the rubbish dumps of industrial society, for his own ends.
Let us not forget, lastly, the humorous and distancing element of the sign at the foot of the central and largest statue,
which reads: "Without Gala and Dalí I would not be here
yet." (The monument near the northern entrance also reveals a favourable critical judgement on Marcel Proust.) There
is a stone fountain next to the central Meissonier, topped
with the hydrogen atom whose meaning we have just outlined in the Pujols monument, originally meant to be a lamp to
light the whole square without the aid of any sort of conven-
tional illumination (we find the hydrogen atom fulfilling this
original function in the Sala de les Peixateries, the Fishmongers' Hall).
While in this square, the visitor should not overlook a sculpture by the German artist Wolf Vostel in the shape of a tower
of fourteen television sets (topped by a woman's head, by
Dalí, with a TV camera incorporated into it to capture the
changing images of the sky, as seen in one of the monitors).
This sculpture rises almost as high as the façade of the Teatre-Museu, and is complemented a few paces away by Dalí's
own "homage" to the monster of the media. This untitled
montage (papier *maché* 290 × 200 × 125 cm) is located in the
entrance doorway to the pavilion used formerly as a fish market and shows a giant's head with a huge and stupid smile,

and a television set (in full working order) in its forehead, on a base of eggs.

Looking up, the visitor will see that the whole of the building is topped by a sort of crown of mannequins. The neo-Palladian architecture of the former opera house of Figueres is thus framed by and contrasted to pieces of *déco* design which Dalí had gold-plated and moulded in synthetic material, so that they would be able to adopt "one thousand eight hundred different positions".

Four figures of "white warrior with loaves of bread on his head" are exhibited along the upper cornice of the former interval hall of the Teatro Principal. The artistic use of loaves of bread, apart from any nutritious function they might have, dates from the period when Dalí created surrealist objects in Paris at the beginning of the thirties. According to Dalí, his image of bread had absolutely no functional or utilitarian meaning, but was rather a symbol of the gratuity and the excess of the free imagination.

We find more figures with loaves on their heads, this time on the balustrade of the balcony of the interval hall of the theatre. These four standing women (casts made from originals by Dalí, 134 × 95 × 20 cm), representing the Fates, with holes in their solar plexuses, holding rather than leaning on the familiar crutches in the form of a hay fork. (Even as a child Dalí insisted that crutches were of most use not to the lame but rather to apparently normal persons; the crutch was also turned into the morphological

Partial view of the Piaza Gala-Salvador Dalí with two of the homages to Meissonier; the montage on the media, in the centre, and the tower of TV sets by Wolf Vostel, on the left.

Installation on the balcony of the main façade: Fates with loaves and crutches (bronze, 134 × 95 × 20 cm), and diver.

symbol of bifurcation.) Finally, on display among the pairs of women is a diver's suit (with a fishbowl on its head), which commemorates a lecture Dalí tried to give in 1936, jammed into a similar suit, on the occasion of the Surrealist International in London. Obviously today, though not so much in 1936, the diving suit is a symbol of the immersion in the depths of the unconscious proposed by Dalí at the time when he was most amazed by, and showed greatest faith in, Freud's work.

Lastly, anyone approaching the museum from the Torre Galatea (the only entrance allowing, due to its more elevated position, a view of Pérez Piñero's latticed dome, the real emblem and trademark of the museum), should remember, when studying the façade covered in triangular loaves of bread and topped by mannequins and huge battlement-like eggs, that it was Dalí himself who in October 1983 planned the alterations in the former Torre Gorgot, rebaptised the Torre Galatea in memory of Gala. The pre-

sence of loaves on the façade is an illustration of his analogical and morphological association of the granulated look of a cauliflower, the breaking foam of waves and some of the decorative elements of Castilian plateresque architecture (the façade of the Casa de las Conchas in Salamanca); with these elements he formulated a new analogical morphology: that of a house whose façade-skin shivers and comes up in "gooseflesh".

THE VESTIBULE AND STAIRCASE. Once the visitor has paid the entrance fee with Dalinian religiosity and has entered the vestibule (opening the glass doors using old irons given the function of handles by Dalí), we think it best to follow the route recommended in the text of this guide (perhaps the neatest tour, or at least the one requiring a minimum of doubling-back), resisting the temptation to head straight into the patio and ground floor of the museum.

The vestibule should be seen as a transitional space which, however, contains (without differentiating here between originals, graphic works and reproductions) some significant reminders of Dalí's world — "Not one single detail of the museum," Dalí repeated, "is the result of improvisation" — basically referring to Picasso, Miró, Gala, the surrealist movement, Dalí's own work and his Teatre-Museu, among other things.

The presence of posters alluding to Picasso and Miró is especially meaningful. Despite their personal differences, more dramatic in Miró's case because of their earlier friendship, Dalí always recognised them as giants of contemporary art, and he wanted to make a statement to this effect once again at the doors of his museum in 1974.

The third notable allusion in the vestibule is to Gala; homage is rendered to her some extent everywhere, here in a phantasmagoric and subtle way in the photo in the centre-left of the *collage*-fan (situated in the opening to the cloakrooms) executed by Dalí's model Amanda Lear under his direction,

*Poster for the opening of the
Picasso Museum, Barcelona,
1977.*

and which Dalí — who was always generous towards his
collaborators — decided to incorporate into his personal Theatre of Memory.

This is in fact the reproduction of a photo of Gala (then still
Elena Diakanoff) in Russia, when she was very young, with
the legend "Tête à château" printed on her forehead with the
turbulent and wilful expression of some exceptional adoles-
cents. (There are two collage-doors to the right and left of a
collage-panel, using a similar technique and also referring to
Dalí's work, all of them executed by Amanda Lear under
Dalí's supervision.)

If we choose the route previously recommended and head
towards the staircase, we see to the left a three-metre crown-
ed eagle. This totemic animal was used in traditional processions. In its breast, where the head of its carrier would have
appeared, Dalí placed a Chinese head as a reminder of and a
homage to the "lost paradises" that surrealist hagiography
located in the opium dens of the East.

Running right up the stairwell, we find one of the most
outlandish montages to be found in the Teatre-Museu. It consists of two fancy dresses designed by Dalí and made in the
early sixties by Christian Dior for a ball in the Beistegui Palace during the Carnival of Venice; Dalí used these costumes to

*Eagle figure for processions,
altered by Dalí and donated by
the group of* castellers *"Els
xiquets de Valls".*

Collage-*fan by Amanda Lear*
under Dalí's supervision for the
opening of the Teatre-Museu.

hide (and to transform into a Dalinian work of art) the brackets of lamps he did not approve of.

All along the lower levels of the staircase, perhaps in the manner of stations of the cross, we find exhibited twelve engravings (51 × 64, and 64 × 51 cm) belonging to the splendid and horrifying series *Carceri d'invenzi*oni (or "The Prisons" by Giambattista Piranesi, 1720-1778), in facsimile editions from the Paris Library. The terrible inner walls of the prisons as imagined by Piranesi are a reminder, besides, of those other aged and scorched walls that made up the ruined shell of the Teatro Principal before it was restored as a museum; Dalí called these walls "marvellous" and even suggested that they not be restored. On the fourth level of the stairway (second floor), we will overlook for a moment the anthropomorphic montage of the doorway, in the shape of a devouring mouth, and turn our attention to the panel (polystyrene and plaster, 450 × 120 cm) with a central column resting along its upper edge and a curtain down the right. This panel is painted black as a background for the white silhouette of a man with a mask instead of a head and a shell over his genitals. The montage was conceived by Dalí for this precise space in his museum, and the white neo-classical silhouette was drawn *in situ* with plaster and the help of a long bamboo cane. On the next wall, and on the same level, we find a large silver-plated head (200 × 180 cm) also on a porespan polystyrene panel; this head was recycled by Dalí from leftover advertising material, although it does recall the silhouettes of large heads installed on the roofs of his Port Lligat home.

Lastly, on the third wall we come to a painting that is representative of one the young Dalí's formative periods. It is an oil painting on canvas done in 1928 (182 × 199.5 cm), similar to a number of compositions in the *Sala de les Peixateries*. Its

Poster for the opening of the
Miró Foundation, Barcelona,
1976.

Ernest Meissonier, Portrait of Napoleon. *Oil on wood, 14 × 11.2 cm.*

title is a little indefinite, having been rebaptised by Dalí himself as *The Fisherwomen of Cadaqués*. It belongs to a period of his youth fraught with conflict and tragedy, after the traumatic ending of his friendship with with Federico García Lorca and before Gala, Paul Eluard's wife, entered his life. Dalí started to reject the most typical iconographic themes of what Santos Torroella has termed "the Lorca phase" (which culminated in the oil painting *Honey Is Sweeter Than Blood*), without having found as yet the characteristic accent of the surrealistic series of paintings grouped around the central work *The Great Masturbator*. This quasi-abstract phase is marked by a rich experimentation with all sorts of materials (especially the sand of Cadaqués and Port Lligat), a certain subtlety of line which allows the influence of Miró's magic to be traced, and, finally, the recurrent themes of the dead bird and (here) a closed fist with one finger outstretched in a clearly phallic allusion.

THE HALL OF THE MASTERPIECES (5th LEVEL).
This hall is situated to the left of the entrance to the passages on the 5th level (3rd floor), right at the end of the staircase. It is the highest part of the museum, containing, in intentional disorder, some treasures from the collection the artist

Engraving in facsimile reproduction from the National Library in Paris of I Carceri *by Giambattista Piranesi, 64 × 51 cm.*

El Greco, St. Paul. *Oil on canvas, 47.5 × 34 cm.*

built up over the years, as well as some outstanding works by Dalí himself. The chronological order of the collection is as follows: El Greco (1542-1614), *St Paul;* Gérard Dou (1613-1675), *The Doctor's Visit* and *The Spinner;* Ernest Meissonier (1815-1891), *Portrait of Napoleon* and *Study of Soldiers;* Adolphe "William" Bouguereau (1825-1905), *Female Nude;* Marià Fortuny (1838-1874), *The Print Collector* and the *Tribunal of the Alhambra;* Modest Urgell (1839-1919), *Cemetery,* and *Untitled;* Marcel Duchamp (1887-1919), *The Suitcase,* a manual series consisting of a box with reproductions and miniatures.

And the Dalís: *Anthropomorphic Bread,* oil on wood, 13.8 × 16.3 cm, c.1932; *Automatic Beginning of a Portrait of Gala (unfinished),* oil on wood, 15 × 18 cm, 1932; *Portrait of Gala with Two Lamb Chops Balanced on Her Shoulder,* oil on wood, 6.9 × 8.8 cm, 1933; *The Saint Surrounded by Three Pi-mesons,* oil on canvas, 42 × 31 cm, 1956; *The Hunter,* oil on wood, 27 × 22 cm, 1956. *Dalí with His Back Turned Painting Gala with Her Back Turned, Eternalised by Three Virtual Corneas Provisionally Reflected in Six Real Mirrors* (non-stereoscopic version), oil on canvas, 62 × 62 cm,

Gérard Dou, The Spinner. *Oil on wood, 24 × 20 cm.*

Marcel Duchamp, The Suitcase, *1938. Box with reproductions and miniatures, 32 × 25 cm.*

Anthropomorphic Bread, *c.1932. Oil on wood, 23.8 × 16.3 cm.*

1972-73; *Hercules and Gradiva* I (text plate); II, ball-point pen and sanguine; and III, sanguine, lead pencil and white *conté* crayon, all 30 × 24 cm, 1973; Untitled I (text plate) 9 × 6.5 cm; and II ball-point pen and sanguine, 24 × 16 cm, c.1973; *Preliminary Study of Gala for the Painting "One Hundred Virtual Virgins Reflected by an As Yet Unspecified Number of Real Mirrors"*, sanguine on plastic, 102 × 153 cm, 1974.

Let it be recalled that the arrangement of all of these works around the hall has nothing to do with chronology, but rather with Dalinian associations of affinity and contrast, and that all of the pieces in this collection are by painters to whom Dalí wished to render a specific homage. In this respect the affinity of Dalí to Marcel Duchamp, the father of the Dadaist anti-artistic revolution is deserving of special mention. The series on display here is a trunkful of artistic (or anti-artistic) reminders of Duchamp, or, as its title implies, a suitcase containing all the items necessary for the artist's journey through life and art. It is, besides, a completely Dadaist manifesto, in that it sets itself up as a portable museum regardless of the orthodoxy and consecratory function of ordinary museums, and elevates reproductions to the category of originals (and vice-versa). Thus fourteen partially visible reproductions are displayed in the glass-case with impeccable Dadaist chaos by Dalí himself, among which we find such emblematic works as *L.H.O.O.Q.* (the famous Mona Lisa with the moustache and goatee, a real "blasphemy" against the religion of art), *Nude Descending*

a *Staircase*, *The Chocolate Mill*, or *The Cemetery of Uniforms and Liveries*, and three well-know miniatures of "ready-mades": the urinal entitled *Fountain* (which is to be viewed, incongruously, in a horizontal position), the Underwood typewriter and the flask containing "50 cc of Paris air".

The value — and visual impact — of Dalí's three works from the thirties on show in this hall is more than obvious. Especially in this period, decidedly realist objects and human figures appear immersed in an atmosphere or space that is luminous in itself rather than lit from a specific source. No exact date has been provided for *Anthropomorphic Bread*, but everything seems indicate that it belongs to a series of phallic loaves executed in 1932 in which the "phenomenal and paralysing bread... symbolises the revenge of an imagined luxury on the utilitarianism of the practical world."

The two miniatures situated to either end of the central glass case are emblematic masterpieces of the post-Freudian phase of Dalí's surrealism. The famous portrait of Gala in the sun in Port Lligat with two lamb chops on her shoulder reveals a paranoiac displacement of the woman who is the object of desire by the raw chops, the appetising promise of a roast that will be devoured in place of the woman. There is a reflection on the edible nature of beauty and the devouring nature of desire at the root of this displacement (witnessed by a girl with her back turned).

Portrait of Gala With Two Lamb Chops Balanced on Her Shoulder, *1933. Oil on wood, 6.9 × 8.8 cm.*

Preliminary Study of Gala for "One Hundred Thousand Virtual Virgins Reflected in an as Yet Unspecified Number of Real Mirrors". *1974. Sanguine on plastic, 102 × 153 cm.*

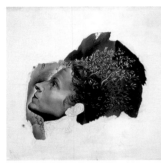

Automatic Beginning of a Portrait of Gala (unfinished), *1932. Oil on wood, 15 × 18 cm.*

Finally, the "unfinished" portrait of Gala refers directly to the benign symbology of the rooted, firm and nutritious olive tree, whose branches spring from the roots of Gala's hair, as a result of the metaphoric association of Gala with the olive tree and the metonymic root of hair-hair-branch. It is worth recalling the astute remark of the critic Cesáreo Rodríguez Aguilera on these two small and extremely meticulous works; he observes that the double Dalinian law "is manifested in condensation and clarity (...) Take a pair of theatre glasses; put the wide end to your eyes; what you see thus is both minute and precise. Analytic mineralisation seems to be the imperative that Salvador Dalí's painting obeys."

Dalí's obsessions of the fifties, a period he himself saw as one of the most fertile in his life, are represented here by two small, intimately inter-related oil paintings. Dalí's painting of the period abandoned the "pure" phase of double images and embarked on another which alternated levitating religious figures and explosions of forms with double or hidden images; simultaneously he composed texts which justified his vision of weightless matter, or matter subjected to centrifugal forces on the basis of his (intellectualised) experience of the "nuclear mystery". In *The Saint Surrounded by Three Pi-mesons*, the corporeal matter of the saint is fragmented in an explosion-levitation caused by the three invisible "pi-mesons". The pion or pi-meson, the lightest of the elementary particles and the essential vector of nuclear energy, was discovered by Yukawa in 1935. The only conceivable concept of God, according to Dalí, was that of an infinitely elemental particle charged with energy: the pion of pions, the vector of vectors.

In this context the title of the second piece in the series, *The Hunter*, may come as a surprise given its non-sacred nature. It shows, literally and directly, the firing of a hunting shotgun, the barrel of which is clearly recognisable in the picture. This gunshot can, however, be interpreted as an initiation, as the symbol of the soul-shock that does away with the spell of the appearances of reality.

Dalí with His Back Turned Painting Gala with Her back turned... brings us to the sixties phase of stereoscopic works, which we will comment on in more detail when we visit the halls devoted to this period in the Torre Galatea, shortly before finishing our visit to the museum. Let us simply observe here that the oil painting exhibited in this hall is not one of a pair (the stereoscopic pair is on display in the Hall of Stereoscopic Paintings in the Torre Galatea), but rather a third work meant to be viewed apart, something which reveals the special value Dalí set on this picture. At the right and left ends of the Duchamp display case we find, respectively, the three pages of *Hercules and Gradiva*, and two pages of another untitled work, illustrating through juxtaposition the process of paranoiac visualisation of virtual images in the mass of letters and blank spaces of a printed text. The untitled work shows the page before the visualization, and then including the sihouetted image; in *Hercules and Gradiva* we see the text, the original drawing and its visualization in the text.

Dalí with His Back Turned Painting Gala with Her Back Turned, Eternalised by Three Virtual Corneas Provisionally Reflected in Six Real Mirrors (non-stereoscopic version), *1972-73. Oil on canvas, 62 × 62 cm.*

Installation created for this space with reproduction of Michaelangelo's Slave, *in plaster and painter black with saddle, c. 1978.*

Finally, we find a 1974 large painting whose technique Dalí defined as "sticky" since it was executed using the prints left on paper (in this case on plastic) by the body of the model smeared in fat.

THE RUE TRAJAN AND THE ANTONI PITXOT EXHIBITION (4th AND 5th LEVELS). As we leave the Hall of the Masterpieces we come to the entrance to the highest of the corridors circling the patio which was formerly the stalls (the 5th level of the staircase, which corresponds to the 3rd floor of the museum). A French street sign gives the name, *Rue Trajan*, to this whole space, here not because it belongs to some famous street, but simply to commeroate the fact that Dalí stole the sign in Cannes in homage to the emperor Trajan, an important figure for him.

The first thing we come to is a montage exemplary for its mixture of logic and disrespect. It is a 112 cm-high plaster reproduction of Michaelangelo's *Slave*, painted in black, with a riding harness. A transparent (slave-black-animal-harness) association that is as scandalous (for anyone unaware of the author's anti-racist sensibility) as it is disrespectful in its manipulation of the original model.

Inside the gallery we find an important selection of graphic work, among which, on the left, it is worth drawing attention to the nine brightly-coloured lithographs, contrasting with the black of the walls (lithographs and engraving on parchment, 77 × 57 cm) for the 1976 edition of the *L'Alchimie des Philosophes;* and entering on the right, the seven lithographs with figures of angels and carriers of crosses, a sun-face, a mouthless face of Gala (most of them 65 × 50 cm) for the edition of the *Twenty Four Surrealist Themes.* It is also worth highlighting the large silhouette cut out of velvet (203 × 77 cm) which reproduces one of Dalí's 1936 "heads with clouds". These works also have the added function of leading us to the most important point in the Rue Trajan: the large window at the right end of the gallery, which invites us to look down on the corridor to the right of the theatre stage.

From this vantage point what we see was one of Dalí's favourite spectacles, according to Antoni Pitxot. Nearest to us we see sacks of coal hanging from the roof which recall the Surrealist International opened on the 17 January 1938 in the Beaux-Arts gallery in Paris, at which Dalí exhibited his famous installation *The Rainy Taxi.* The montage for the halls was originally Duchamp's idea, who conceived a route through a darkened cave, which the visitors would have to follow using torches. From the roof of the cave sacks of coal were hung like giant bats, reproduced here in the museum in a clear Dalinian homage to Marcel Duchamp.

Immortality, *from the series* L'Alchimie des Philosophes, *1976. Lithograph on parchment, 77 × 57 cm.*

The Phoenix, *from the series*
L'Alchimie des Philosophes,
1976. Lithograph on parchment,
77 × 57 cm.

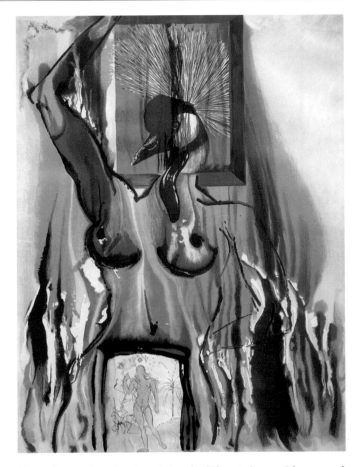

If we descend to the fourth level of the stairway (the second
floor of the museum), we are met by the *Anthropomorphic
Mouth* (310 × 250 cm) which swallows visitors to the
permanent exhibition of paintings by Antoni Pitxot (a
montage which, because of its structure and materials, is a
variation on the head surrounded corn cobs, 170 × 80 cm,
situated inside). In the reception hallway, to the left,
Mnemosine (oil on canvas, 194.5 × 96.5 cm, 1979) mother of
muses, by Antoni Pitxot, gives us an emblematic welcome.
Dalí wanted Pitxot's exhibition to be opened at the same
time as his Teatre-Museu, and for it to be installed
permanently in this corridor, only subject to alterations and
incorporations specified by Pitxot himself.
The relationship between the Dalís and the Pichots went back
a long way. Indeed, Dalí's father, Salvador, decided to take up
his practice as notary in Figueres to be near his schoolmate
Pepito Pichot. Years later the Dalís would spend their sum-
mers in Cadaqués, following the example of Doña Antonia
(that admirable woman who managed to turn all seven of her
children into artists). Outstanding among them were Ramón,
the impressionist who led a bohemian and slightly ascetic life
(Ortega y Gasset rebaptised him "*Quichot*"), Ricardo, the violinist who gave Dadaist concerts avant la lettre to the animals

on his farm, and who was Antoni Pitxot's father, and Pepito, who had the gift of making orchards bear fruit and gardens bloom and who was, according to Dalí, the most artistic of the children. It was Pepito who accompanied Dalí in an open carriage to convalesce in the Torre del Molí, where the child took the firm the decision to become a painter, and what is more an "impressionist" painter, and where "the most artistic of the Pichot brothers" showed the historical good sense to take him seriously. It was also Pepito who introduced the young Dalí, before he left for the Residencia de Estudiantes in Madrid to the radical literary and aesthetic language of the Italian futurists. But the artistic reunion of Dalí and one of the Pichots was not to come about until August 1972, when Dalí visited Antoni's studio; Antoni was the nephew of Pepito and Ramón and the son of Ricardo, the cellist. When he saw Antoni's work (the young painter had adopted the original spelling of his surname, Provençal according to the poet J. V. Foix), Dalí took the decision to incorporate it into his plans for the Teatre-Museu.

Pitxot's work is above all a treatment of stone matter (the stones from the beaches and coves of Cape Creus), considered in itself the object of a "microscopic" analysis, which is at the same time an analogical symbol of the macrocosm. Pitxot's stones, what is more, fuse the atemporality and hardness of the mineral kingdom with the softness and temporality of their coloured mouldy covering. Finally, Pitxot's creative process leads him to anthropormorphize his universe of stones into ever more complex sculptural and scenic unities, increasingly loaded with allegorical meaning.

Antoni Pitxot, The Allegory of Memory, *1979. Oil on canvas, 220 × 210 cm.*

In the smaller rooms and the two wings of the corridor on this level we find an extensive collection of works which are representative of the ever more allegorical creative process of Antoni Pitxot. This process perhaps culminates in the piece entitled *The Allegory of Memory*, an oil painting (220 cm × 210 cm, 1979) which is also notable for its special position in the small room in the left-hand gallery of the corridor that led to the theatre boxes. *The Allegory of Memory* belongs to the series "the caves" (or fantastic interior scenes) and the *Mnemosines* (a mythological figure who symbolises memory, the basis of all creative intelligence, and also therefore the nine muses).

THE MAE WEST CORRIDOR AND HALL. We now arrive on the 3rd level of the staircase (the first floor of the museum) and resist the temptation to turn left on the corridor (we will do this later); instead we continue the visit along the right-hand gallery which contains very significant installations, and which leads to the Mae West Hall and subsequently to the stage and lower levels of the museum.

In the entrance hall on this level we find a *Venus de Milo With Drawers*, a reproduction of the famous 1936 plaster original (98 × 32.5 × 34 cm), designed by Dalí and executed by Marcel Duchamp. On that occasion Dalí declared his wish was to set the "drawers of conscience" inside a body still ignorant of the Christian invention of guilt, so that his sculpture would act as a cure for "the sickness of psychoanalysis". The copy on display here belongs to a 1964 bronze cast painted to make it look like plaster. Dalí's original idea was for the visitors to strike the sculpture with a spoon and be surprised by its unexpected metallic sound.

After the Venus we come to three lithographs from Calderon's *La vida es sueño*. Then to a smaller room containing four plastic bubbled or three-dimensional op-art pieces (127 × 50, 102 × 45, 101 × 50, and 50 × 35 cm, respectively), created with the aim of inspiring visions or "apparitions", possible of a religious nature. They are thus no more than a humorous example of Dalí's passion for optical illusions seen as the source of phenomenological reflection. The installation is complemented by an untitled oil painting on plywood (183 × 100 cm, c. 1978), with its neo-classical themes. This painting was executed quickly, maybe even in one day, but certainly on a day of high spirits in Port Lligat, marking a brief parenthesis during a specially tragic period in the life of Salvador Dalí.

Next, after an engraving from the *Gargantua and Pantagruel* series and an illuminated stained glass work by Francis Gruber (Nancy 1912- Paris 1948), we come to the first of three important glass cases along this gallery, featuring Dalí's "hypercubic" crosses from the fifties. These crosses are in part a product of his reflection on the levitation and fragmentation of spritualised matter; it must not be forgotten, however, that the cube represents the *logos*, and that by articulating logos-cubes Dalí seemed to be tracing a Christian

Engraving from the series Gargantua and Pantagruel, *1973, 76 × 54 cm.*

Retrospective Bust of Woman, 1970. Reproduction of 1933 original. Painted bronze, 70 × 54 × 35 cm.

cross with somewhat rationalist connotations. Along with the photograph of the *Corpus Hypercubicus*, a classical (or "pagan") sculpture, inverted and decapitated, and the small hypercubic cross (40 × 30 cm) in olive wood which served as a model for the *Corpus Hypercubicus*, we find another cross on display in the case (120 × 90cm, and 90 cm deep on its double cross-pieces), whose cubes are covered with plastic mirrors. However, the most important feature of this spectacular work is its capacity for articulated movement, which always leaves its structure in a (symbolic) position of instability or impossible balance. The whole, according to Dalí, was meant to illustrate the "fall of paganism and the triumph of Christianity."

In the second of these showcases Dalí created a multicoloured space containing ornamental elements from the world of the spectacle, violently contrasted with two anti-artistic sculptures: *La Fleur du Mal* (an *assemblage* in glass, plastic and metallized paper, with one paraffin wax foot and another rather disgusting foot of the type used for anatomy study) and the *The Immortality of Castor and Polux* (metal version of an illustration from *Dix Recettes d'Immortalité* with the ana-

Michelangelo figure with drawer in its forehead, originally executed as an illustration for the walls of the stage of the Teatre-Museu. Oil on wrapping paper, 178 × 140 cm.

Venus de Milo with Drawers, *1964. Copy of the original designed by Salvador Dalí and executed by Marcel Duchamp in 1936. Bronze with plaster patina, 98 × 32.5 × 34 cm.*

tomical reproduction of the anus of two Siamese twins, one with fifty-two grooves around its sphincter, the other with fifty-three, their only differentiating feature.

The third case, also featuring a background of pheasant feathers, contains a very important piece. It is a 1970 reproduction, with slight changes, of the 1933 *Retrospective Bust of a Woman* (70 × 54 × 35 cm). In the 1970 cast, the whole bust (except for the necklace with its drawings of figures) is executed in painted bronze, whereas in the 1933 original the bread and the ears of corn were natural, which explains Dalí's comment on the imaginative and completely non-utilitarian function of the bread, in the sense that nothing could be easier than to jam the feet of an inkstand into a loaf, and nothing could be more beautiful than to see the bread softened and stained with ink blots. *Retrospective Bust of a Woman* thus contains many of the most characteristic iconographic elements of Dalí's work, such as the spindle-shaped loaf on the figure's head, the ants which represent the (sexual) Dalinian phobia of decomposing matter attacked by carnivorous insects, and the ink-stand with the reproduction of Millet's *The Angelus*, a theme we will treat in more detail later on. Among other elements included in the case, the "virtual" cup with its real spoon (which reminds us not so much that reality has a double-meaning, but rather, inversely, that we see reality where there is none); and the sculpture of the Bust, made up of a black-gloved hand which clasps (or struggles with) a white paraffin wax hand, representing the racial problems which Dalí witnesses during his time in the US, and which he "denounced" in his 1943 *Poetry of America.*

Let us now go on to the Mae West Hall: once we pass through the arcade which overlooks the stage, a titan seems to be throwing a (real) pillar at us from the lateral wall (under the above-mentioned roof of sleeping bats-sacks of coal) as a welcome. For this large stage space Dalí painted, with intentional simplicity, a whole series of titans in the manner of Giulio Romano's giants, used to illuminate the large halls of the Tea Palace in Mantua.

The Mae West Hall applies Dalí's well-known double-image technique to the furnishing of a room in *The Face of Mae West That Can Be Used As a Drawing Room* (c. 1934-35), which the artist achieved by retouching and colouring in *gouache* a photograph published in a newspaper. The intention was thus to provoke a three-dimensional reading from a two-dimensional image, while in the Teatre-Museu, the visitor is invited to do exactly the opposite, that is, to read a three-dimensional space in two dimensions.

At the beginning of the seventies Dalí got to know the Barcelona architect and designer Óscar Tusquets, author of a new version of the *Sofa-saliva-lips* (or *Saliva-sofá*) in red spongy fibre (the first production was carried out in pink satin, as a commission from Edward James, in 1936). Tusquets followed Dalí's specifications and carried out the project in 1974 with the help of the architect Pedro Aldámiz. Dalí also retouched the photo enlargements of two pointillist

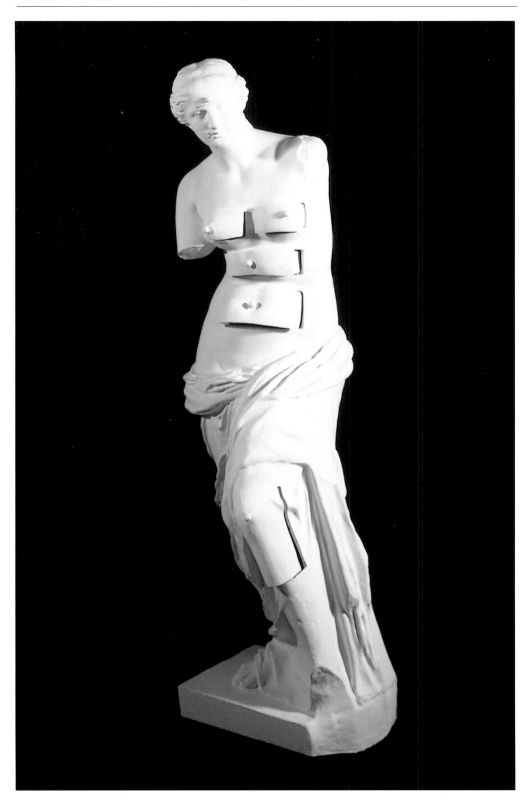

pictures of Paris (oil on photograph, 129 × 299 cm) which make up the eyes of the actress, had the nose moulded in a factory in Olot, inserted "burning" trunks into the nostrils, commissioned the Llongueras hairdressers to make the wig from natural hair to frame the face; above all, he amused himself with putting together the baroque *assemblage* of the nose, collecting objects of the "worst good taste" that he could he find (a mantelpiece clock, a Venus and fans). In order to solve the problem of perspective Óscar Tusquets, because of the difficulty in laying down a floor that would slope gradually downwards to the viewer, ingeniously decided to have the whole background lean slightly backwards. However, it was Robert Descharnes who had the idea of having the visitor stand in front of a reductive lens, while Dalí thought of placing the small stairway leading to the lens behind a plastic camel recycled from the advertising paraphernalia of the Camel company. The whole thus acquires the surprising and disquieting connotations of a fairground attraction, which Dalí enhanced in 1977 by placing a variety of bathroom objects upside down on the roof of the Mae West installation.

We find a number of extremely significant works on the walls of this room. As we enter, there are two oil paintings on canvas to the right by Silvère Godéré, the Rouen hyperrealist painter, executed in 1975 on Dalí's request only in greys, reds and sky blue. The first (72.5 × 100cm) is a copy of *Les énervés*

Side view of the Mae West *installation by Salvador Dalí and Óscar Tusquets, 1974. Three-dimensional version with* gouache *on advertising photo, 1934-35.*

Óscar Tusquets, Scfa-Saliva-Lips *(or* Saliva-sofa*), early seventies. Red sporgy fibre.*

de Jumièges by E. V. Luminais, a work with a pre-Raphaelite air which illustrates the legend of two brothers hamstrung by their father and abandoned in the Seine as a punishment for their incestuous relationship with their mother. This copy is one of a pair; the other was an advertisement for Canon (92 × 60.5 cm), executed in the same tones, which Dalí had hung in an off-horizontal position, thus alluding to the silhouette of the brother's boat. Another Silvère Godéré on the next wall copies the cover of a record by Duke Ellington. (In this respect, it is well to remember that the American hyperrealist and *pop* painters, Andy Warhol chief among them, never disguised their debt to Dalí's anti-informalist crusade.) Thus, on the same wall we see on display a portrait of Dalí (pencil on paper, 39 × 32.5 cm) executed from a photo by Sebastián Cestero in 1975.

Between this portrait and the reproduction of the cover of Duke Ellington's record, there are two Dalí works which manipulate neo-classical themes: one is a 1973 bronze with white patina, 155 cm in height, in the shape of the Venus de Milo with drawers, a crutch and a giraffe neck; and an oil pointing on plywood (201 × 122 cm) of the sculpture of a hairy mother-creature feeding its child. Under the staircase topped by the camel we find a *pop* montage in plastic and fabric with Japanese figures (71 × 58 cm); on the other side of the staircase there is a plaster sculpture (96 × 45 cm) of the monstrous figure of a discus thrower under a violinist, in turn under a hippopotamus, all of them topped by a smaller version of the "virtual" cup commented on above.

Next come one of the oils on paper (194 × 134 cm) executed by Dalí so that they could be cut out by his collaborator Antoni Pitxot and installed under Pérez Piñero's dome. On this occasion, however, given the subtlety of its lines, it was

Figure with Turban, *c. 1978. Oil on paper, 190 × 120 cm.*

Otorrhinological Head of Venus, *1965. Painted plaster sculpture, 60 × 30 cm.*

decided not to exhibit it uncut. On the third wall, facing the entrance, we come first to a glass case with a 1981 version of his *Otorrhinological head of Venus* (60 × 30 cm) in white and sky blue, with an ear instead of nose, and a nose instead of an ear, a representation of the delirious freedom of a synaesthetic metaphor (attribution of the qualities of one sense to another). To the left of this Venus there is another oil on paper (194 × 134 cm) which would be impossible to exhibit in the natural light of the stage. Further on again, we see the *Mannequin-Chair*, a 1976 sculpture, 181.5 cm in height, composed of heterogeneous elements, meant by Dalí, according to Descharnes, as a homage to the anthropomorphic figures created by the eighteenth-century Florentine painter and engraver Giovanni Battista Braccelli. Next we come to another large ornamental oil painting (178 × 140 cm), a version of a Michaelangelo with a Dalinian drawer in its forehead; the last piece hung on this wall is a 24 cm mask with a top hat, again with drawers, conceived, illustrated (with Duchamp's moustached Mona Lisa and the portrait of

Helen Rothschild) and worn by Dalí at one of the Rothschilds' fancy-dress balls.

On the next wall (just above the broken table, a piece executed and donated in 1973 by the Catalan film director Bigas Luna) there is an oil painting on canvas (100 × 100 cm), considered representative of Dalí's peculiar version of some of the postulates of cubism in 1926 and 1927, a period marked by the friendship and influence of García Lorca. The critic Rafael Santos Torroella has identified this work as the *Harlequin* exhibited for the first time in Dalí's second exhibition in the Galeries Dalmau in Barcelona, allowing it to be dated c.1926. Often given the title *Head of a Woman*, it was later called *Amoeba Face* by Dalí.

On the other side of the Mae West stage we see that the screen closing off the side of the leaning background installed by the architect Óscar Tusquets has two vertical orifices in it. Dalí decided that, since people like to queue up, the screen was to be holed at two levels (at the adult and child eye level) so that curious visitors would look through it; Dalí's declared intention was to put "anything at all" inside the screen. (This "anything at all", pretty much Dadaist in aim, turns out to be *Bed-fountain*, a landscape overlooked by a sink which has the poetic function of a full moon).

To the left of these slits for looking at "anything at all", Dalí placed a hyperrealist work of his entitled *The Trial of Mary Dugan* (oil on canvas, 104 × 130 cm), meant to make us believe that we are viewing not an oil painting but a photograph. Next, on the wall which brings us to the exit, this hyperrealist series is complemented by a photograph which looks like a painting (*Fhotographic Composition of a Nude*, 108 × 158

Silvère Godéré, copy of the work by E. V. Luminais, Les énervés de Jumièges, *1975. Oil on canvas, 72.5 × 100 cm.*

Amoeba Face, *1926. Oil on canvas, 100 × 100 cm.*

cm), which cannot definitely be attributed to Dalí, and, finally, by a poster for the 1974 Dalí exhibition of the Daniel Hechter collection.

In the outer corridor we come, on the right, to the installation glimpsed from the look-out point on the Rue Trajan; it can now be seen that the old woman dozing and rocking in a chair (a plaster piece by the Catalan hyperrealist sculptor Francesc Anglès) is tied with a sort of red umbilical cord to the only unreal cube in the installation, painted on the roof, and that the festival masks executed in Port Lligat in memory of, or at least as a reference to, the Canary Island painter Nestor Fernández have red bulbs in their eye sockets, like bloody pupils. This installation is complemented by a number of objects: a huge lamp from the Casino Sport, a recreational club in Figueres; a standard made of a loaf of bread, the skull of a sheep; a copy (250 × 165 cm) of *The Bath of the Faun* by Borguereau, a painting with a mythological theme which shows a group of solicitous nymphs setting upon a faun apparently badly needing a wash (for which the installation provides plenty of buckets of water); and finally, one of the anthropomorphic seats (white, 240 cm in height) designed by Dalí for the garden of his house in Port Lligat, which finishes off the installation on ground level and pairs off with the chair by Doctor Anglès; the seat can almost be interpreted as an anthropomorphically transmuted version of the old woman and her chair after their fall from the level of the corridor (and also from the level of dreams).

UNDER THE GEODESIC DOME. Dalí had wanted the stage of the former Teatro Principal to be covered by a latticed transparent dome by Samuel Fuller, though it was in the end the Spanish architect Emilio Pérez Piñero who took charge of the project and became Dalí's friend and collaborator up until his death in a road accident on 9 July 1972. Basically, the design Dalí and Pérez Piñero aimed at in their plan for the exhibition spaces under the dome, in order to seal these spaces from the outside without breaking the visual continuity of the open sky with the stage, on the one hand, and the courtyard, on the other, which would continue exposed to the open air. The dome should also be interpreted as a gigantic sculptural illustration of Dalí's reflection on one of his obsessive themes: that or morphological analogies, recreated thanks to the paranoiac-critical method. Thus the geodesic dome is not merely an obvious image of the world (a world whose surface is transparent so that interior and exterior universes can communicate); it is also only conceivable in relation to the latticed image, augmented by the microscope, of the compound eye of a fly (an insect which, in general, represents the Dalinian polar opposite of the disgust caused by locusts, grasshoppers and ants).

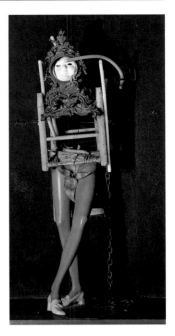

Mannequin-chair, *1976. Assemblage with mannequin's legs, wicker chair, clock casing and chain.*

The setting in place of the dome caused new aesthetic problems because Dalí did not approve of the brusque way the stone of the wall met the supporting vault. He thus decided to paint a false red latticed structure on a blue ground on the underside of the supporting vault, and to crown the meeting of the supporting vault and the latticed dome with sixteen plaster sculptures (from 60 to 130 cm) executed in Port Lligat, representing the "guardian angels" of the museum. While the work on the supporting vault was being carried out, some blue paint splattered the stone of the wall and was immediately transformed into a spectacular Dalinian work: the top of the wall was painted with dark trickles dripping from some kind of eruption of blue, while on the right-hand wall (facing the patio) a nude titan with a cubic head (oil on plywood, 339 × 679 cm) is wringing the a blue sheet, while on the left-hand wall two huge hands are holding up (or dropping) a white sheet. (Other giants from the same series are on display in the open spaces of the walls).

If we lower our gaze again we see, just on the vertical of the lateral arcades, the niches of the former stage machinery in which Dalí housed five slightly larger sculptures (140 cm.) than those belonging to the same thematic series crowning the dome. Tapestries showing bullfighting scenes are exhibited below the the statues, and hanging from the vertices of the arches; in these scenes Dalí makes a theme and technique apparently typical of Picasso into something of his own.

We can now turn our attention to the background painting covering the whole wall facing the plate glass window (880 × 1300 cm) glue on canvas, after an original by Salvador Dalí for his fourth incursion into the world of the stage: the ballet *Laberinto*, which opened in the Metropolitan Opera House, New York, in October 1941, with a libretto, scenery and cos-

Side view of the stage and entrance to the Sala del Tresor, to the right. Above, the "chance" splatters of paint and Titan, *c. 1978.*

tumes by Dalí. This spectacular canvas shows a desolate human figure with an egg-shaped head whose cracks foretell a hatching, also seen in the right-hand image of *The Metamorphosis of Narcissus*, 1936-37, in a floral renaissance of the mythological character. Apart from the striking hole in the breast of this figure, in the form of a door leading inwards, it is worth highlighting the Dalinian association of "chest hair" and a tree or bush set on the solar plexus of the figure, as well as the fact that the bright light illuminating the very slightly emphasised facial profile of the figure throws a shadow that is not only very violent, but also impossible.

Another of the most spectacular pieces to be found on the stage is housed in the right-hand corridor, so that it can be viewed with the right perspective from the opposite corridor. It is the large oil on photographic paper (420 × 317 cm) entitled *Gala Nude Looking at the Sea, which, at a Distance of Eighteen Metres, Is Transformed into a Portrait of Abraham Lincoln (Homage to Rothko)*. The conception of this work is a result of a cybernetic application of the Dalinian obsession with the double image, as a proposed reflection on the relativity of the point of view of the spectator. The face of Lincoln was painted on the basis of a digital interpretation by the cybernetic expert Leon D. Harmon, and appears in a small format reproduction to the left of Gala's calves. She is also reproduced, in a slightly different pose, to the left of the small portrait of Lincoln. Less easily noticeable is the splendid refer-

ence to *Christ of St. John of the Cross* (1951) which floats in the heights of a glorious sunset. It must be pointed out, finally, that the choice of the figure of Abraham Lincoln, the president who abolished slavery, cannot be seen as gratuitous. Nor that the painting should be dedicated to the US painter Mark Rothko, who died in 1970, and whose worked evolved from surrealism to the psychologistic use of a few elementary colours.

To the left of the plate glass wall separating us from the patio we find a large oil painting (298 × 200 cm), executed during the summer months between the years 1970-74, entitled *Ruggiero freeing Angelica*, which alludes to and parodies the painting of the same name by Ingres. Here the monster Ruggiero and his horse have been ridiculously reduced in size; the lance (which in both Ingres and Dalí distributes the spatial tensions of the canvas) has been turned into a laser ray; and Angelica has become the undisputed protagonist of the work, Dalí maliciously chose his friend Amanda Lear, with her provocatively sexual beauty, as his model.

On the right of the window a tapestry reproducing one of Dalí's most complex works from the end of the sixties, *The Hallucinogenic Toreador*, has been rehung. This large oil painting (398.8 × 299.7 cm), painted from 1968 to 1970, contains a great number of the iconographic elements and phenomenological reflections typical of Dalí's work and inaugurates the explicitly tragic tone of his last works. In this

Side view of the stage with the entrances to the Mae West Hall, centre (first level), and the Sala de les Peixateries, left (lower level).

Background for Laberinto, *1974. Copy of 1941 original. Glue on canvas, 880 × 1300 cm.*

painting a Palladian bullring (devastated by uncountable fly-corpuscles which make up the image of a bullfighter toasting the spectral face of Gala and that of the dead bull), is the tragic scene of an obsessive repetition of the Venus de Milo, which, in turn, contains the image of a bullfighter shedding a tear on receiving a premonition of his own death, while the child Dalí watches all of this, from the past, on the rocky landscape of Cape Creus.

Just under the tapestry of *The Hallucinogenic Toreador* we find another product of Dalí's collaboration with the architect Pérez Piñero, in the form of a mobile sculpture made up of a folding metal structure, a small face painted by Dalí in oils, and rags. When the whole is folded, it looks like nothing more than a ball of rags. As the structure unfolds it makes up a kind of latticed spider's web from which a Christ figure appears, with its arms extended. Dalí's intention was to surprise the spectator with this appearance of Christ from nothing.

To the right of this folding sculpture we find a montage in the shape of an alter with another of the least figurative Christs produced by Salvador Dalí. This is the 1976 *Twisted Christ*, a 125 cm-high sculpture in white plastic wax and a cross in copper-plated tin. The titles refers to the pose of the figure, an effect reinforced by the rope which ties it to the cross the multiple reflection in the dihedrallly-shaped mirror behind it. Anyone familiar with the photographs of Antoni Gaudí's sculptural studies for *La Sagrada Familia* in Barcelona will immediately recognise the explicit homage render-

Gala Nude Looking at the Sea, Which , at a Distance of Eighteen Metres, Is Transformed into a Portrait of Abraham Lincoln (Homage to Rothko), *1976. Oil on photographic paper, 420 × 317 cm.*

ed by Dalí to Gaudí the sculptor, who introduced the technique of multiple visualisation. This installation also holds a hidden surprise. Hardly visible between curtains we find another installation which allows us to see, reflected in a mirror and faintly illuminated, an oil painting measuring 225 × 163 cm, entitled *Explosion of Mystical Faith in a Cathedral.* Dalí wanted this painting, which shows faith exploding like fireworks, to be displayed in such a way that (perhaps like real faith) it would only be found by those who really looked for it, and that even when it was glimpsed only those who were familiar with the original work would be able to understand that they were being offered a spectacular, reversed and false reading of it.

Finally, to the left and in a space between the pillars of the second arcade, we find displayed an original work (ink and *collage,* 64 × 46 cm, 1973) showing Saint Narcissus (who miraculously caused a plague of flies to attack the French army of Philip the Brave), and, in the centre, a sculpture from the years 1974-5 (210 × 140 cm), which brings together heterogeneous elements in a biographical homage to a pair of gypsies who played their organ under the balconies of the city when Dalí was a child. To the right of the third arcade we find another of the ink-smudged or "sticky" works (sanguine, 150 × 100 cm, 1970) which Dalí executed in the manner

Explosion of Mystical Faith in a
Cathedral, *c. 1974. Oil on
canvas, 225 × 163 cm.*

of Yves Klein, who made this technique fashionable in the fifties.

And let us not overlook the tombstone of Salvador Dalí set in
the pavement of the stage. It is a very discrete tombstone
which signals the vertex of the crypt which we will visit
later.

"SALA DEL TRESOR" (THE TREASURE HALL). To
the right of the stage (still facing the courtyard), between the
pillars of the third arch, we fund the entrance to the Treasure
Hall, which we will visit now in order to avoid doubling back
later.

It is worth recalling that Dalí did not want to display his
works (which we will comment on in a counter-clockwise
direction) in chronological order. Thus, we come first to the
Self Portrait Split in Three (oil on canvas, 71.1 × 511 cm,
1926-27), which deserves to be compared to the *Amoeba
Face* (or *Harlequin* or *Head of a Woman*) mentioned above.
If the structure of the triple silhouette is identical in both,
the radicality of meaning and colour in the *Self Portrait*
seems however to indicate that we are dealing with a slightly
later work in which, according to Santos Toroella's sugges-

Self Portrait Split in Three, *1926-27. Oil on canvas, 71.1 × 51.1 cm.*

tive theory, an allusion to Federico García Lorca and to the prefiguration of the monstrous profile of *The Grand Mastur-bator* is evident and explicit. We now come to *Siphon and Bottle of Rum with Cork* (oil on canvas, 79 × 49 cm, 1924), one of the rare examples or exercises in the mode of the Italian metaphysical school of Carlo Carrà and Giorgio de Chirico that Dalí painted at the Residencia de Estudiantes in Madrid.

The next work is definitely representative. Dalí never display his panicked phobias of sexual passion as strongly as in *The Spectre of Sex Aappeal* (oil on wood, 18 × 14 cm, 1932), initially entitled *The Spectre of the Libido*, in purely orthodox Freudian fashion. In this painting on olive wood, Dalí gives shape to his terrible vision of the female sex, against the atemporal and geological background of Cape Creus: the image of a woman without a head, hands and feet propped up in its chaotic monumentality by crutches. Its breasts and belly appear as mere sacks containing some kind of nutrient, perhaps necessary, but never beneficial. The horror, however, stems from the age of the spectator, the unmistakable child figure of Dalí dressed in a sailor suit (holding a femur instead of a stick for his hoop), the real protagonist of the

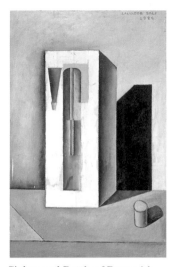

Siphon and Bottle of Rum with Cork, *1924. Oil on canvas, 79 × 49 cm.*

work. This is the illustration of more than one vague sexual ghost, experienced since childhood and presenting sex in a coercive fashion as the most mysterious and repugnant of sins.

Let us now return to 1924 with *Purist Still Life* (oil on canvas, 100 × 100 cm), probably painted in the Residencia de Estudiantes, and in which the young Dalí offers us his peculiar vision of "purism", in fact a neo-cubism indebted to Juan Gris. It was included in his first individual exhibition in the Dalmau Gallery in Barcelona in 1925.

The first of the portraits of Gala we come to in this hall is an ink and *gouache* on cardboard executed in 1969, "taking advantage of the stains on the paper". It is a remarkably skilful exercise, outstanding in Dalí's opus, in that it portrays his muse with a rare smile. We are then offered one of his "double visions" evolved according to the paranoid-critical method in 1938. The work is given the title *The Image Disappears* (oil on canvas, 55.9 × 50.8 cm), an allusion to the reading and discovery of the second image which impedes our vision of the first, and which contains obvious references to *The Reader* by Vermeer, and whose outline appears in Velasquez's face. We then come to a 1974 drawing (graphite pencil on paper, 28 × 34 cm) which associates the morphology of a horse with soft feminine forms, comparable in

The Spectre of Sex-Appeal, *1932. Oil on canvas, 18 × 14 cm.*

their theme, execution and intention to the well-known 1935 pen and ink study for *Suburbs of the Paranoiac-critical City*.

The famous 1944-45 portrait of Gala entitled *Galarina* (oil on canvas, 64.1 × 50.2 cm) deserves special mention because during its slow execution Dalí saw himself as Raphael painting Fornarina. On one occasion Dalí compared this *Gaiarina* to his 1945 *The Basket of Bread*, in that Gala's naked left breast, cradled in her own arms, is similar in composition to the bread in its basket. If the association between these two masterpieces is not explicit, then the similarity in colouring, and the light which last seems to emanate from the bread and the breast rather than from outside, certainly is. Although it does show obviously the deep relationship linking the artist and the model, this portrait can strike the viewer slightly disquieting. Dalí himself declared that if one looks at this portrait for a long time, "in the end it frightens you..."

Purist Still Life, 1924. Oil on canvas, 100 × 100 cm.

After *Galarina*, and continuing the proposed associative reading of Dalí, we come to the 1945 version of *The Basket of Bread* (oil on canvas, 33 × 38 cm), which must be seen as the real treasure of this hall. Finished in California a day before the end of the Second World War, it was put on show for the first time in the Bignou Gallery in New York and made such an impact that it was selected as a graphic emblem for the Marshall Plan for economic aid to Europe after the war. This fact is symptomatic in that, by accepting it, Dalí seemed to be distancing himself from the intention (the pure expression of a non-utilitarian imagination) of the first *Basket of Bread*, painted in 1926. The perfect and, at the same time, impossible realism of this painting (the light emanates from the very energy of matter, not from any external source) is an affirmation of the fact that we are dealing with a total enigma, expressed in terms of "stereoscopic hyper-aestheticism". Dalí was also categorical in his declaration that this oil painting was "most rigorous from the point of view of geometrical preparation. (Its) structural tensions are pushed to their limit." It should be pointed out, by way of an anecdote illustrating the painter's predilection for this work, that Dalí refused to hand *The Basket of Bread* over to any transport company for its journey to Figueres, but kept it with him all the way.

Of the various paintings that have Gala as their model, the next we come to is of special interest; *Atomic Leda* (oil on canvas, 61.1 × 45.3 cm), 1949, is perhaps an illustration of

The Image Disappears, 1938. Oil on canvas, 55.9 × 50.8 cm.

Gala Nude From Behind
Looking in an Invisible Mirror,
1960. Oil on canvas, 41 × 31.3 cm.

the fact that after *The Basket of Bread*, the "corpuscular explosion", or the levitation and suspension of spiritual matter, had really taken place. In the last analysis, as Dalí himself perceptively commented, this work constitutes a challenge to the inevitability of death ("Even death itself rises from the earth..."). Two other works with Gala as their model come next: *Gala Contemplating the Corpus Hypercubicus* (oil on canvas, 31 × 27 cm, 1954), which is a study for the said oil painting; and *Gala Nude from Behind Looking in an Invisible Mirror* (oil on canvas, 41 × 31.3 cm, 1960), in which Dalí involves himself in the nude back of his model while she is narcissistically occupied with the contemplation of her own body in a mirror that is not included in the pairing.

Let us now go back to 1935-36 to view *Singularities*, an oil on wood (40.5 × 51.1 cm, c. 1935-36) which is completely typical of the Dalinian surrealism of the period. Just look at a the monstrous figure on the right of the painting which seems to be the pictorial manifestation of the "huge hairy rottenness", Dalí's words for Àngel Guimerà in his scandalous "Moral Position on Surrealism" lecture, given on 22 March 1930 in the Ateneo Barcelonès.

We now jump further back in time, to 1924, with *Port Alguer*,

The Basket of Bread, *1945. Oil on canvas, 33 × 38 cm.*

an oil on canvas (100 × 100 cm) which has been popularised in endless reproductions. The young Dalí who painted this picture had already made his first incursions into cubism and was thus in a position to manage, technically, an analysis of the "cubic" architecture of Cadaqués modelled on the example of Picasso and the *Noucentistes*. In order to paint this landscape, now so well-known, Dalí, who had a studio on the seashore, decided to bring his easel out into the open air. There is a photograph of Dalí painting *Port Alguer*. The young artist is wearing an aproned overall that covers him to the ankles, and a battery of paintbrushes are tied with cords to his belt so he could use one or other of the brushes according to the colour required at the moment, and then leave it drop again, without wating time. The second Cadaqués landscape that we come to is a bright seascape (oil on canvas, 31 × 34 cm, c.1920-21), in which the theme of the white sail crossing the Bay of Cadaqués appears, a typical image which would continue to appear in the background of his marine paintings until 1923-24. We now have the chance to view a small oil study on wood (18.5 × 23.5 cm, 1962) for *The Battle of Tetuan* containing the group of four horsemen which, in the finished work, is seen to the left of Gala forming double and triple images. On the bottom left-hand corner of this study there is an affectionate dedication: "For Gala, guiding light of my life, Dalí 1962".

The penultimate work in the hall is another oil painting on wood (61 × 38 cm), which cannot be definitely dated (c.1922-24), entitled *Portrait of Ramoneta Montsalvatge*, a woman known in the Figueres of Dalí's youth for her strong personality, which transgressed the limits of the bourgeois canons of the time. It is odd all the same that the portrait should have remained unfinished; this is perhaps a deliberate act since, as it is, the picture exerts an extreme fascination. Our visit to the Treasure Hall ends with *Villa Pepita*, an oil on canvas (48.4 × 50 cm), which can also only be dated approximately (c. 1921-23), and in which the young Dalí indulged in a very suggestive exercise loaded with allusions to Matisse among others. The sign of the name of the town should be noted for its incorporation of words into a work of this period.

"SALA DE LES PEIXATERIES" (THE FISHMONGERS' HALL). We now go back across the stage to descend to the lower level of the museum and the important *Sala de les Peixateries* (thus named because it had been the municipal fish market of Figueres). Some paintings dot the wall on the short way to the hall: the first is an oil on plywood (79 × 139.2

Galarina, *1944-45. Oil on canvas, 64.1 × 50.2 cm.*

Singularities, *c.1935-1936. Oil on wood, 40.5 × 51.1 cm.*

cm) with the image of the face of *The Night* from the tomb of the Medicis, by Michaelangelo (cracked and slightly slanted by Dalí to create a feeling of unease). Next we come to a *Head of Beethoven* (184.5 × 139.6 cm), a work representative of the Dalinian theory of the artistic manipulation of chance in that it is the result of a public performance by Dalí in 1973, in which he used his feet to retouch the ink traces that two live octopuses left on Bristol board.

The main feature of the hall is the predominance of works from the period of youthful apprenticeship and experiment, and of, at the other end of the chronological scale, works from the latest period, with the exception for those on display in the central chamber, where it is advisable to start our visit. This chamber is overseen by an atom (in the form of a lamp) of hydrogen, evidence of Dalí's obsession for the spiritually regenerative potential of contemporary science, but also of his 1952 vision of the finitude of the universe in the form of a *continuum* made up of four female buttocks.

To the right of the interior of the central rectangle we find the *Soft Self Portrait with Grilled Rashers of Bacon* (oil on canvas, 61.3 × 50.8 cm, 1941) which is typically "anti-psychological" in intention: the soul of the artist has no interest (perhaps no existence), only its wrapping (the skin) deserving to be analysed. As a result this skin is necessarily "soft" (and held up with Dalinian crutches) and "edible" (it is already being devoured by those heralds of decay, the ants); although he is human, his condition is in no way superior to that of the slice of bacon that appears on the pedestal.

Facing his *Self Portrait* Dalí hung his *Portrait of Picasso* (oil on canvas, 64.1 × 54.7 cm, 1947). This work is in no sentimental accommodation. From the perspective of the new classicism proposed by Dalí in those years, his visionary view of the genius of Picasso is ambivalent and critical. Intellectualism, sentimentalism, a new entusiasm for folk art and the exaltation of ugliness seem to be, for Dalí, the main elements making up Pablo Picasso's exceptional creative personality; Dalí usually thanked Picassso for having evolved and exhausted, in a few decades, a process of "destruction" of art that without him might have gone on for centuries.

In the two lower glass cases we have, to the left, the stereoscopic work entitled *The structure of DNA* (oil on canvas in two 60 × 60 cm panels). In the seventies Dalí experimented pictorially with a third hyper-realist dimension, producing double images, slightly modified and provided with Wheatstone mirrors, one for each eye. On the right, on the other hand, Dalí takes on a more ambitious exercise. What

Head of Beethoven, *1973.*
Octopus ink and sanguine on paper, 184.5 × 139.6 cm.

Soft Self Portrait with Grilled Bacon Rasher, *1941. Oil on canvas. 61.3 × 50.8 cm.*

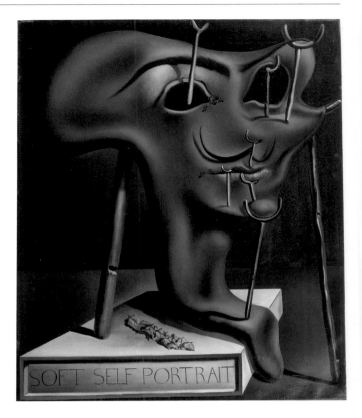

he aims at is for the viewer to be able to combine his pointillist recreation of a painting by Raphael with the opposite half of the second painting, thus creating a new image on the retina: *Athens Is Burning!* (oil on canvas in two 32.3 × 43 cm panels, c. 1979-80), part *The School of Athens* and part *The Burning of Borgo*, with the help of Bela Julesz's anaglyphic structures. The central space of the whole is overseen by alternating works, such as *Rhinocerontic Figure of Phidias Illisos* (oil on canvas, 100 × 129.5 cm, 1954).

Among the most outstanding works on the walls of the hall, which we will comment on in anti-clockwise, we come first to the *Satirical Composition* (*gouache* on cardboard, 138 × 105 cm, 1923), in which the musicians on the left seem to have appeared from the universe of Chagall, except that one of them is playing a huge pear instead of a violin (and in a slightly wrong posture). Next comes the famous 1923 *Self Portrait* (oil, *gouache* and *collage* on cardboard, 104.9 × 75.4 cm) evidence that at this time Dalí already knew and practised the principles of the Italian and French avant-gardes. This painting includes a collage of the French communist newspaper *L'Humanité*, of which, to the horror of his family, the young Dalí, the eternal provocateur, was the only subscriber in Figueres.

On the three outer walls of the central chamber we find a very interesting monographic display of the short creative

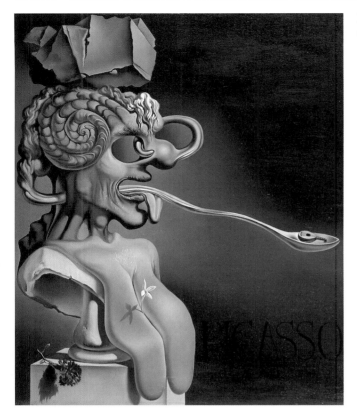

Portrait of Picasso, *1947. Oil on canvas, 64.1 ×54.7 cm.*

period covering the artist's search for a definitive identity in the years 1927-29. The influence in this series of the iconograms of Miró and of a certain atmosphere indebted to Max Ernst has been highlighted by certain critics. Dalí, however, leaves his personal mark in the shape of rotting birds or animals and symbols (in general clearly phallic fingers), and also the experimental use of gravel and sand from Port Lligat and Cadaqués. This is the work of a tormented period of Dalí's life, during which his art seems to grope along different paths such as pure abstraction and the symbolically figurative *The Great Masturbator* (which, from 1929 on, would mark the tendency which won out in this struggle).

The first piece on show on the outside right-hand panel is *Moonlight* (oil and sand on wood, 63.1 × 75.7 cm, c. 1928), a work in which Dalí pushes abstraction and experimentation with materials to the extreme. The second is the emblematic *Woman-animal Symbiosis* (id., 50.2 × 65.5 cm, 1928), which is notable for the presence of small rotting zoomorphic figures. Let us recall that this theme of "decay" was given a literary formulation by Dalí in 1927, in the famous poem-manifesto, in which the hard and anti-sentimental aesthetic of St. Sebastian was opposed, in art as much as in life, to the "decay" of subjectivity.

On the extreme left of the front wall what is considered the best work of his neo-cubist period is exhibited: *The Barcelona*

Rhinocerontic Figure of Phidias Illisos, *1954. Oil on canvas, 100 × 129.5 cm.*

Self Portrait, *1923. Oil, gouache and newspaper on cardboard, 104 × 75.4 cm.*

Mannequin (oil on canvas, 198 × 148 cm, c. 1926-1927), which illustrated one of the first articles in the Catalan press devoted to Dalí, in February 1927. In the painting the characteristic triple outline of the heads of this period is extended to the whole right-hand profile of the body (whose feminine attributes do not prevent the inclusion of a fish-phallus at the level of the genitals).

We then come to two oil paintings belonging to Dalí's latest period, 1982 to be precise; they alone are enough to dispel any suspicions of the painter's creative exhaustion in these tragic years: *The Pieta* (oil on canvas, 100.2 × 100 cm) and *Othello Dreaming of Venice* (id., 99.8 × 90.2 cm). They are typical works by the old master who, at the age of 78, achieved very ambitious goals with an economy of resources imposed by age. In his version of Michaelangelo's sculpture it could well be said that the real protagonist is the image of a calm and natural death. If it is true to say that Dalí's work is always autobiographical, here we are dealing with the manifestation of a premonition, perhaps stemming more from the senses than the intellect, of the experience of death. *Othello dreaming of Venice* is a piece that is even more filled with nostalgia, if that were possible: the chin of the dying man is blurred with the trembling of some impossible desire; but his memories are unclear and evanescent, while the geological reality of death is clearly outlined in the hole in his breast. The last work, on the extreme left of this wall, is *The Road of the Enigma* (oil on

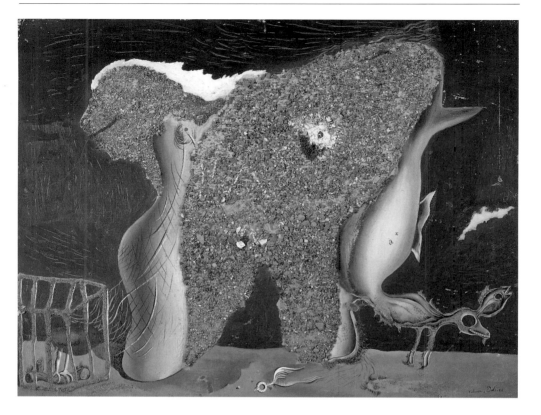

canvas, 139 × 94 cm, 1981), a work whose structure reproduces or reminds us of the famous surrealistic composition (later called *Inaugural Gooseflesh*), 1928, as if Dalí were closing a life cycle or returning to his first "officially" surrealist work.

On the outside panel of the central rectangle parallel to this wall we find, once again, two representative works from the critical 1927-1928 period just referred to. They are two striking untitled paintings whose meticulousness and carnality suggest they belong to the *Cinderella* (1927-28) creative phase.

The first painting we come to on the left-hand lateral wall is *The Happy Horse* (oil on wood, 122 × 244 cm), whose title can be nothing other than an expression of a terrible sarcasm, since it is a reflection of the serious illness Dalí was suffering in 1980, from which he would recover to return to the theme of death (*The Pieta and Othello*) in another spiritual and artistic mood.

Let us now study a 1966 sculpture *Lilith-Homage to Raymond Rousell* (plaster with paint and forks, 152 × 60 cm), in which two half Victoria of Samotracia figures are joined by a bloody crack with a mat of hair resembling a vagina or armpit (let us recall the impact of this image in *Le Chien Andalou*). The historical character of this monster with a demon's name is emphasised by the presence of two Napoleonic horsemen in bronze by Meissonier.

A variety of paintings in cardboard from Dalí's youth follow,

Woman-Animal Symbiosis, 1928.
Oil on wood with sand,
10.2 × 65.5 cm.

The Pieta, *1982. Oil on canvas,*
100.2 × 100 cm.

with their popular, folk, or festive motifs, which should be
seen as exercises in the assimilation of the Catalan symbolist,
impressionist and rustic-traditionalist masters. The left-hand
wall of the hall normal exhibits *Dawn, Noon, Evening and*
Twilight (with which we conclude our visit to this hall), some-
time replaced by *Raphaelesque Hallucination* (oil on wood,
122 × 244 cm, 1979), a landscape with a figure after Raphael,
in which the artist allows himself to be led by the grain of the
wood.

Facing this wall, on the outside of the central space, we find,
once again, two works from the period monographically treated on these three panels: the first of these is the central *Rot-*
ting Bird (oil on canvas, 37.5 × 57 cm, 1928), in which an
atmosphere of devastation recalling *Honey Is Sweeter Than*
Blood is created.

Some of the works temporarily installed in this space (and
which may return to it in the future) deserve our utmost
attention. For example the study (oil on canvas, 71 × 96.5
cm, 1944) for the background scenery of the ballet *Mad Tris-*
tan, based on music by Wagner and choreography by Lionide Massine; or the oil *collage* on an advertising image *Baby-*
Mapa-Mundi (49.5 × 38.5 cm, 1939), executed at the height
of the paranoid-critical phase and in which the visionary

Barcelona Mannequin, *c. 1926-27.*
Oil on canvas, 198 × 148 cm.

Dalí shows the map of Africa for the first time dripping blood; but even more important from our point of view is *Dawn, Noon, Evening and Twilight* (oil on wood, 122 × 244 cm), a piece executed for Dalí's exhibition in the Pompidou Centre in 1979. In this large picture, Dalí involves himself in a meditation on the relativity of time, on the one hand paralysed in the ecstatic moment of prayer (being said by the devouring mother of Millet's *Angelus*) and, on the other, caught in its flux by means of light and space (but light and space which are pure vibrations captured with a pointillist technique). Dalí reinforces this formulation of relativity by tracing an impossible shadow of the sun in discord with the rest of the shadows, and supplying a short but striking taped soundtrack, written by him, which goes "What's the time?" "It's time for the Angelus" "Then bring me a harlequin!"

Dawn, Noon, Evening and Twilight, *1979. Oil on wood, 122 × 244 cm.*

THE LOWER LEVEL: THE HALL OF DRAWINGS, THE CRYPT, THE CORRIDOR AND THE PATIO.

As we leave the *Sala de les Peixateries* we turn left to begin our tour of the lower level of the Theatre-Museum in the following order: the Hall of Drawings, the crypt, the semi-circular corridor which circles the patio, whose ramp will allow us to climb again onto the stage to head for the steps, on the right, which lead up to the first-floor corridor and the final stages of our visit.

The Hall of Drawings brings together a varied (and chronologically confused) selection of Dalí's talents in all sorts of paper media (pencil, charcoal, India ink, *gouache*, water-colour, washes and sanguine), as a fitting testimony to the Dalinian obsession with mastering a craft which for him would have been unthinkable without fluency in drawing and old sorts of other expressive techniques.

Of the twenty or so originals on paper exhibited here, the quality of the three realist portraits of Gala is worthy of mention; situated on the right-hand wall of the Hall they

Project for the Dematerialisation of Nero's Nose, *1947. India ink on paper, 53.5 × 37 cm.*

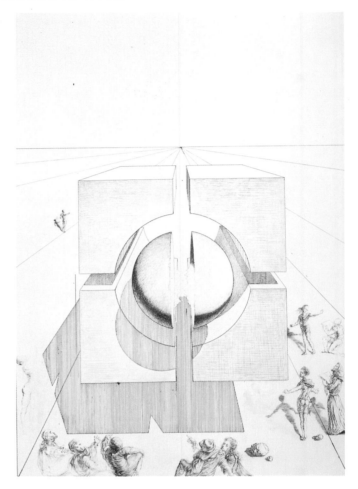

are the 1926 *Study for Ana Maria Sewing* (53 × 32.4 cm); *Study for a Portrait of Gala with a Turban* (pencil, 52 × 32.4 cm), 1939; and a *Foreshortened Gala* (43.4 × 35.7 cm), 1952. Also to the right we find a study in India ink (53.5 × 37 cm) entitled *Project for the Dematerialisation of Nero's Nose* (study for *The Splitting of the Atom*), 1947; and a study in charcoal (33 × 32 cm, c.1933-34) for *Atavistic Dusk*, a new version of Dalí's terrifying reading of the unmistakable iconography of Millet. Finally, to each side of the door leading into the crypt, we find two versions (India ink wash, both 63.5 × 48.5 cm) of the double image *Metamorphosis of the Bust of a Man in a Scene Inspired by Vermeer*, 1939.

On the facing wall (which allows access to the patio corridor) two very interesting 1941 illustrations are on display which were to be used in the design and editing of the dream sequences of a film (the project was rejected by the producers). They show the double image of a pair of café talkers who turn into a skull (pencil, wash and India ink on cardboard whitened with *gouache*, 13.6 × 12.6 cm), and the *Face of War* (pencil, wash and India ink, 17.05 × 13.2 cm)

Study for a Portrait of Gala with Turban, *1939. Pencil on paper, 52 × 32.4 cm.*

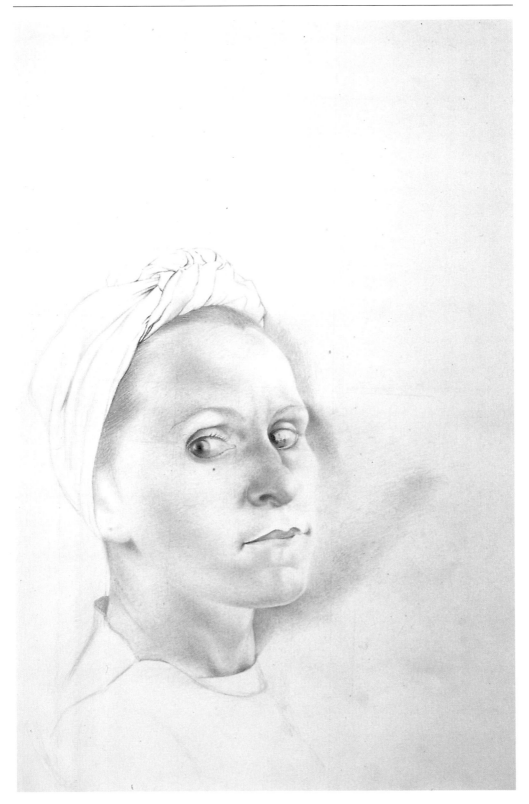

First Cylindrical Hologram,
Portrait of the Alice Cooper's
Brain, *1973. Pastel and sanguine
on paper.*

which suggests an association of images mingled in a fratricidal crowd, a spider's web and a honey comb or wasp's
nest, while in the opening of the mouth the image of the
face itself is reproduced ad infinitum (thus constituting a
slightly altered version of the 1940 oil painting of the same
name).

Of the works situated on the left-hand wall, we would like to
call attention to an example of Dalí's capacity for transforma-
tion in the 1973 study entitled *First Cylindrical Hologram,
Portrait of Alice Cooper's Brain* (pastel and sanguine on
paper, 30 × 41.5 cm) he decontextualizes and gives sense to
the silhouettes (taken from a newspaper photo) of two foot-
ballers involved in a game; and a splendid study in pencil,
wash and India ink (38.7 × 58.7 cm) for an advertisement for
the perfume "Désert", which shows a woman embracing a
stone figure of Narcissus in a barren landscape; the bulb-
head of the figure has already flowered (notice that the
fusion of the two characters only takes place in the their shadows).

Access to the crypt is by way of the hall we have just mentioned. It is a small chamber occupied at one end by the Figueres
tombstone reading "Salvador Dalí i Doménech. Marquès de
Dalí de Púbol. 1904-1989." As Dalí did not leave, on his death-
bed in the Torre Galatea, any written clarification of his wish
to be buried in his museum, it must be assumed that this fact
stemmed from his pathological terror of the gloomy crypt in
the castle of Púbol (where Gala is buried) and from the
equally pathological desire to remain somehow in close con-
tact with life, represented here by the visitors to his Theatre
of Memory.

The remaining walls of the crypt hold a good proportion of
the original cut-outs of angels and titans originally executed by Dalí in order to decorate the walls of the stage.
There are seven large compositions on wrapping paper and
wood, with violent and tragic giants and angels inspired in
Giulio Romano's enormous figures, and perhaps also in
those of Luca Cambiaso (a painter who Dalí praised for his

"cubic" figures and for dying completely mad in El Escorial in 1585).

Back in the Hall of Drawings we turn right into the entrance to the corridor which leads around the patio (and former stalls of the theatre), where a surprise awaits us in the form of the cover of the magazine *Pour Vous* (45 × 30.4 cm, 1939), with the double image of a face of the aviator B. Stockfeld and the squat outline of a woman seated on the ground (which very much recalls the image of the Wet Nurse Llúcia, immortalized five years before in *The Weaning of the Furniture-Nutrition;* and the advertising print (51 × 45 cm), retouched in 1942, also with *gouache* and India ink, as an illustration of the ironic association between bourgeois interior decoration and a stable full of sheep and hens.

Dalí wanted to hold, along the corridor and up to the entrance to the open-air patio, a permanent exhibition of the work of his friend, the painter Evarist Vallès, of whom he wrote (as appears in his own hand, with a few typical spelling mistakes, at the exit to this section to the corridor): "Vallès is the only painter to have sunk a hatchet into the sky of the Ampurdan." The thirty or so works by the artist exhibited here, and the three display cases containing his very personal sculptures in pink-coloured resin, give a notion of the different phases of his work.

Continuing along this corridor we come back to Dalí's work, this time in the form of four installations placed in niches, as well as twenty-two engravings (76x 54 cm) from the Rabelaisian *Garçantua and Pantagruel* series for the 1973 edition.

The first niche we come to is an installation showing a simplified wooden version (120 × 40 × 50 cm) of the famous 1960 bronze which reproduces a wicker chair with spoons. The chair is flanked by two plaster Venuses and the whole is overseen by a bronze (65 × 19 cm) which gives shape to the "erotic" dream Dalí once had on a summer night in 1966: the

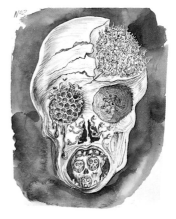

The Face of War, *1941. Pencil, wash and India ink on paper, 17.05 × 13.2 cm.*

Struggle of Giants, *1977. Oil on wood, 123 × 245 cm.*

Tristan and Isolde, *1944. Oil on canvas, 26.7 × 48.3 cm.*

View of The Car-naval (carnival) *of culture, on the walls, the crown of sinks "monster fountains" by Dalí and Pitxot and modernista street lamps; in the boxes, art-déco mannequins, Olivier Bricè's* Venus velata, *the* Homage to Braccelli *sculpture in chains and the installation with a suit by Paco Rabanne and a crocodile skull.*

monstrous vision of a being with a goat's skull for its head and an anthropomorphic violin body. The second case displays a selection of cabinet mouldings (in which Dalí perceived the double image, outlined in fibre-tip pen, of a smiling person), and an oil-painting and *collage* with a cuttle-fish shell (17 × 12 cm), with an Arab figure in relief. The next niche deserves our minute attention, for it contains two important works from 1944: the gloomy oil on canvas, executed for a piece of scenery for *Tristan and Isolde* (26.7 × 48.3 cm), and an oil and *gouache* (100 × 78 cm) showing a surprising version, filled with light and happiness, of *The Great Masturbator* (valuable, also, in that it constitutes one of the very few references to this work among the pieces contained in the Teatre-Museu). The first oil painting, carried out as a study for the scenery of Lionide Massine's ballet, fuses the visionary reading of the Wagnerian characters with the mother and son of *The Angelus* of Millet, thus relating the heroic myth of impossible and fatal love with the Freudian Oedipus Complex in a devastated and arid landscape. The installation contained in the fourth and last niche possibly has its origin in pure chance: the peculiar presents Dalí received from his admirers. This is certainly true of the small dried crocodile, transformed into a two-footed lamp 110 cm in height, as well as of the orthopaedic leg of a bullfighting picador from Figueres, from which Dalí made a mannequin with a crocodile face. This display case also contains a soft watch (bronze, 11 × 35 11 cm), on a blue background with a starfish and octopus legs.

If we double back a few we enter the former stalls of the theatre by way of the right-hand wing of the corridor, to come face-to-face with the spectacular installation made up of The Rainy Cadillac with a statue by Ernst Fuchs (bronze, 260 cm in height) set as an ornament on the front of the bonnet, the column of tractor tyres topped with the marble statue by

View of the patio with the Rainy Cadillac *installation.*

François Girardon, a reproduction in black of Michaelangelo's slave, and Gala's boat, with very large crutches, a black umbrella and very large drops of sea-water. The symbolic force of this montage, according to Dalí, was rooted in the figure of Queen Esther in the act of dragging the chains of the "cart of culture" (a cart he also described as "*car-naval-esco*").

The first and emblematic version of *The Rainy Taxi* was created for the International Exhibition of Surrealism in the Beaux-Arts gallery in Paris, in January 1938. This is in fact its fourth version, using the Cadillac the couple had driven in from coast to coast a number of times during their stays in the USA. In this version it naturally rains inside as well as outside the car. The third spectacular element of this installation is Gala's boat, from which large drops of sea-water hang (the mould for which was obtained using condoms filled with water). If we lift our gaze we see (besides the crown of white polyester sinks, 80 cm in height, and the recurrent figure of twenty-one golden art-déco mannequins) four niches in which are displayed, from left to right, a *Venus velata* by Olivier Bricè, 200 cm in height, a silhouette (190 × 90 cm) made with a bronze chain in 1982 entitled *Homage to Braccelli*, a metal suit (125 cm) by the fashion designer Paco Rabanne and finally the reproduction, this time upside-down, of the *Homage to Bracelli*. The Egyptian mannequin and the central doorway are framed by a pair of street lamps (310 cm) by Hector Guimard from the Paris Metro (saved by Dalí when the Paris city authorities destroyed almost all of these historic pieces), which Dalí has resting on a base of fossil snails from the Pyrenees. We now see, between the large central windows of the patio, the four sculpted *Grotesque Monsters* (some of which reach 600 cm in height), made by Antoni Pitxot with the help of the Grenada builder Benito López, from Dalí's initial idea. These are four anthropomorphic shapes, in the manner of the "grotesque" monsters of Florentine gardens, through whose mouth water pours. The sex and anthropomorphic symbology of the monsters alternates, and they are made with materials of the most diverse origins imaginable.

Let us remember, lastly, that the scenography of the patio, according to Dalí, would only be whole and complete with the mixture of a backing track he chose for it (alternately Wagner and *The Mystery of Elche*) with the deep and ancient bells of the neighbouring parish (where he was baptised).

"PALAU DEL VENT" (PALACE OF THE WIND).

Back on the first-floor of the Teatre-Museu, we head now to the *Palau del Vent* (Palace of the Wind). Facing its entrance we find, among others, an interesting lithograph (66 × 41 cm) with a portrait of Picasso (relatively young and adorned with the glorious laurels of an *Empereur*, as Dalí himself underlines), to which the painter added a small ink sketch.

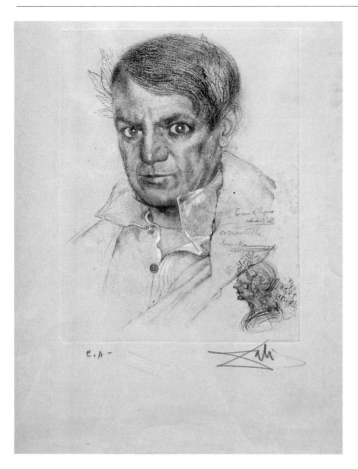

Portrait of Picasso (I have also met the emperor), *1970. Lithograph, 66 ×41 cm.*

The Palau del Vent (the former foyer of the theatre) is made up of a central hall with three smaller rooms off it, which make up, according to Dalí, the basic living spaces (studio, bedroom and living room) of an artist's home. In the central space or great hall our attention is drawn to the ceiling mural: an oil painting on canvas pasted to the plaster of the roof, begun in 1972 in Port Lligat and finished in situ on scaffolding in 1973 (1100 × 575 at the base 840 × 235 on the roof). The name of this space refers to the plain of the Ampurdan, the ideal setting for the mythical visit of the winds, especially the tramontana. All in all the vision of the Ampurdan offered by Dalí in this painting is one of tranquillity, luminosity and abundance. The central body of the painting offers a foreshortened image of Gala and Dalí, deified and ascending into heaven. There is a touch of Dalinian humour in the fact the foreshortening leaves us with huge feet and barely visible heads. On the right-hand side, Gala and Dalí reappear, with their backs to us, gazing at a civilised, inhabited landscape with — even more important — obviously mystical connotations, overlooked by the enigmatic symbol of a polyhedral structure. On the opposite wall we are offered a compendium of all of Dalí's iconography (*The Great Masturbator,* soft watches, elephants with mosquito's feet, etc.) accompa-

Self Portrait, *1921. Oil on canvas, 47.5 ×31 cm.*

Between the two entrances to the "Workshop" chamber the Study for Galarina, *1943; right, the bronze* Bust of Velazquez *with double images, 1974; right and at the end, inside the "Workshop", the easel with the oils* Galatea of the Spheres, *1952, and* Portrait of Gala with Rhinocerontic Symptoms, *1954.*

nied by a rain of gold which (thanks to the painter, who hardly accidentally chooses this spot to sign his name) descends on the inhabitants of the Ampurdan in the middle of a sardana dance. The side panel over the entrance door is reserved, on the other hand, for History, with a tally of the peoples who settled in the region. The fourth side panel is overseen by a Christ crucified, and his shadow, levitating over a bare landscape (in the bottom left-hand corner of which we find the figure of Dalí's friend, the photographer Melitó Casals, whose visit to the painter gave birth to the creation of the museum).

To the right and left of the door to the outer corridor we find, respectively, the *Headless and Armless Female Torso* (70 × 50 cm) and the *Head of Christ* (60 × 50 cm), two 1972 *sfumatos*, executed on paper burned with candle smoke and *gouache*, slightly retouched with the fingers.

A display case facing the access contains the two-cornered hat, the frock coat and a facsimile of the sword Dalí wore in his inaugural session as a member of the French Academy, on 9 May 1979, in recognition of his very considerable body of essays and literary work, a good deal of it written in French. Above the case we find an oil painting from the early eighties on plywood (120 × 240 cm), framed with canvas shoes and imitation cherries. This *Allegory of Spring* without doubt evokes the first still life of cherries he painted (and real maggots extracted for the cherries that served as models) so much

admired by Pepito Pichot, and thanks to which Salvador, the boy who wanted to be a painter, embarked on his "genius" life.

Between the entrance doors to the "bedroom" we find the famous 1921 *Cyclopean Self-portrait* (oil on canvas, 47.5 × 31 cm) executed in Figueres when he was seventeen. Under this is exhibited an installation made up of two gold castings (*Perseus Beheading the Medusa* and a Christ crucified without a cross), as well as a miniature (oil on wood, 9 × 12 cm), entitled *Path in Púbol*, from the early seventies. All of this is supported on a table formed by the (inverted) adaptation of *Lilith or The Double Victoria of Samotracia*. We now enter the Bedroom through the right-hand door, where the first thing to catch our eye is the strange bed with its seashell-dragon legs (230 × 160 × 50 cm), commissioned by Napoleon III and apparently found in one of the most exclusive and reputable brothels of the old Paris. Not by chance we find right beside the bed a golden gorilla skeleton (170 cm high) with a reproduction of the head of *Saint Theresa* by Bernini (33 × 23 cm) on its chest (with her cheeks covered in sores and maggots): the symbol of the animality closest to the *homo sapiens* is here clothed in glorious gold while the ecstatic spirituality of the mystic reveals its carnal condition in the process of putrefaction.

The central piece of this space should not cause us to overlook the interesting collection of small sculptures set on

View of the central hall with the entrances to the "Bedroom". On the ceiling, the foreshortened image of Dalí's feet ascending into heaven; below centre, the 1921 Self Portrait; left, bronze casting of the original Homage to Newton.

Brothel bed, golden gorilla skeleton and tapestry with a reproduction of The Persistence of Memory, *left in the "Bedroom".*

Shoe and Glass of Milk, *1975. Reproduction of 1932 original (destroyed).*

the different levels and cases of the large modernista sofa-sideboard (85 × 386 × 35 cm) on the right-hand side of the Bedroom, on the back-rest of which Dalí painted a whole Ampurdan landscape. On the central section of this piece, starting at the top, we find among other provocative para-noiac-critical sculptures a seagull with half of its body made up of Michelin tyres, and a slightly modified 1973 version in porcelain of his 1934 *Hysterical and aerodyna-mical Female Nude* (46 × 26 × 15 cm), in which Dalí "hyste-rically" incarnated the morphological principles of aerody-namics into a female body, thus creating an aesthetically decorative and morally perverse (in other words, *Art Nou-veau*) irrationality; just to its right there is a small (25 cm) gilt bronze reproduction of the *Homage to Newton* and another bronze, this one black and slightly larger (30 cm), with its torso bulging and deformed. A clutter of objects is found on the shelf of the left-hand mirror, with the "Miche-lin" monster once again outstanding, this time with the head and neck of a swan, while two extremely significant works are on display in the left-hand case: the first, a 50 cm. vase showing a modernista Leda seduced by a ridicu-lous duck which incarnates and brings together the convul-sively provocative condition of all the pieces on show here; the second, below, is a 1975 47 × 23 cm reproduction of the

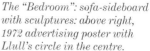

The "Bedroom": sofa-sideboard
with sculptures: above right,
1972 advertising poster with
Llull's circle in the centre.

very famous 1932 (destroyed) *Shoe and Glass of Milk*, a
surrealist object with a symbolic function made up of a
variety of accessories; if the sugar cube on which a shoe
has been painted were to be dropped into the milk the shoe
and the cube would disappear.

Let us not forget, in this space, Dalí's large poster for
the French National Lottery (1972) on which he later
superimposed *Llull's Wheel*, a 100 × 100 cm oil painting
whose radical optical combination of green and red aimed
at "petrifying" the viewer. Indeed, the enlargement, in the
centre, of one of the coins reveals the false and petrifying
nature of gold, and in its centre we glimpse the deadly face
of the Medusa. Finally, there is a tapestry (300 × 460 cm)
over the bed with drawings inspired in the arabesques of
printed circuits, which frame a reproduction of his crucial
The Persistence of Memory (1931). (Dalí conceived and
executed these very famous soft watches in Paris in a
single afternoon; when Gala studied the painting a few
hours later she insisted that anyone who saw it would
never forget it.)

If we come out of the Bedroom by the entrance flanked by a
copy of the 130 cm bronze casting of *Homage to Newton*, we
enter a gallery of the main façade. Here, on the right, there is
a large photo-reproduction (245 × 194 cm) of then Prince Juan

Study for Galarina, *1943. Lead
pencil on paper, 72.3 × 53.7 cm.*

Study for The Hallucinogenic Toreador, *c.1968. Oil on canvas, 57.5 × 44.5 cm.*

Carlos, executed in Japan using a serial enlargement technique: to the left of the reproduction the image of the prince appears again, highlighting Dalí's defence of reprographic techniques, rooted in the provocative aesthetic of Marcel Duchamp.

This gallery is given the name "Ten recipes for immortality" because a number of engravings and two copies of the book-carrying case from the 1972 series of the same name. Opposite the protrait of the prince, the carrying case (64 × 48 × 10 cm) constitutes a small installation of its own: its gilt-engraved perspex covers have fried eggs for their locks and telephone receivers for handles; between the covers a small golden structure with a polyhedral centre has been placed, like a throne with a high back-rest whose image is multiplied in the inside mirrors.

On the partition wall of the central space a series of six lithographs (65 × 50 cm) from *Homage to Quevedo* is exhibited, surrounding a relief featuring an image of Quevedo belonging to the original theatre. This medallion is, incidentally, connected by a sort of umbilical cord to an electronic circuit board, under which we see a 1980 oil on plywood, *Setting Sun* (of a slightly distorted rectangular shape, 30/34 × 118/117 cm), which because of its aim, style and date must be paired with the gloomy oil paining *The Happy Horse*, mentioned in the *Sala de Peixateries*.

When we leave the gallery to enter the "Workshop", we find the *Bust of Velazquez* (90 × 60) transforming itself into three chatting figures, a 1974 bronze on whose face (27x 26 cm) Dalí superimposed the double image of woman with head-dress (on the chin and mouth), two faces with a throat (on the eyes) and *Las Meninas* (on the forehead). Between the two doors of the Workshop is displayed an Alexandrine warrior by D'Alonso which rests, in turn, on a base of inverted Victoria of Samotracia figures. Just above this we find the splendid 1943 *Study for Galarina* (lead pencil on paper 72.3 × 53.7 cm), in which Gala, bejewelled, adopts a slightly more solemn position than in the oil painting exhibited in the Treasure Hall.

The Workshop as a whole was dedicated by Dalí to the "eternal female", with its representative works of nineteenth century realism, surrealism and hyper-realism. An important oil study is exhibited by the right-hand entrance (c.1968, 57.5 × 44.5 cm) for the *Hallucinogenic Toreador*, centring around the main figure in the Venus de Milo and the face of the bull-fighter. Beside it we come to other Bouguereau from Dalí's collection (180 × 94 cm), which shows a female nude pulling a thorn from her foot. Looking up we see an optical illusion (*The Golden Goat of the Castle of Carmansó*, 122 × 244 cm,

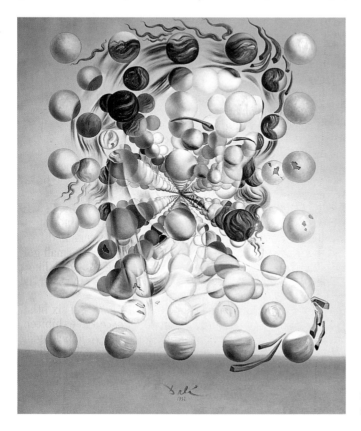

Galatea of the Spheres, *1952. Oil on canvas, 65 × 54 cm.*

Portrait of Gala with
Rhinocerontic Symptoms, *1954.*
Oil on canvas, 39 × 31 cm.

1979), with a nude woman resting on spirals which if stared at for a time, start to look like gold coins, Dalí thus wishing to impose a reading of gold as falseness or a mere optical illusion.

We come next to Meissonier's easel, (with a telephone incorporated) on which are displayed two portraits of Gala: the splendid 1952 *Galatea of the Spheres* (oil on canvas, 64 × 54 cm), a wonder of technical precision, imagination and delicacy, and which even Dalí himself called the "paroxysm of joy". *Gala with Rhinocerontic Symptoms*, just below, was painted two years later (39 × 31 cm), in which the blooming of matter (here in the form of logarithmic rhinoceros horns) takes place only in the flesh of Gala dicolletage, "at top speed". In addition, a theatre curtain (450 × 500 cm) by the Catalan impressionist Meifrén, hangs along the wall facing the entrance.

On the adjoining wall we find an installation made up of a large romantic oil painting by an unknown artist (317 × 225 cm), which Dalí had pierced with two matador's swords, and two large wood an perspex doors with a geometric drawing consisting of the strings of fourteen canvas shoes and a pair of handles (100 × 15 cm) in relief (cire-perdue on bronze, forming a sinuous mass of female nudes). Finally, between the two entrances to the drawing room we find a 1972 pencil drawing (39 × 50 cm), with horses and women carrying jars, and, in French, the phrase "Drawn to amuse Gala".

Two sculptures overlook the central space of this chamber dedicated to the "eternal female": a bronze head representing *Fortune*, whose serpent's body is made up of 720 teaspoons which descend from the ceiling describing three turns of a spiral, and a 1972 life-sized hyper-realist nude (165 cm in height) in "anti-artistic" polyester, by the Californian sculptor John de Andrea.

POETRY OF AMERICA, THE CORRIDOR AND HALL OF JEWELS. Turning left on the corridor as we leave the *Palau del Vent*, we come to a a display case given over to Millet's *Angelus*, a painting which gave rise to one of Dalí's most spectacular and penetrating paranoiac-critical reflections of the early thirties (published in 1963). It involves the development of a Greek tragic, Oedipal and even cannibalistic interpretation of Millet's very well-known picture, which Dalí incorporated obsessively into his own work. Dalí did not see an image of calm and piety in these two peasant figures apparently saying the Angelus together; he saw death, incest and devouring, this second reading, of which viewers of Millet's painting are unaware, being the key to the popular fascination it exercises. No reader of Dalí's essay can fail to see in the mother a religious mantis ready to devour the male, and in the son an Oedipal victim trying to repress and control his passion (the erection he covers with his hat) and his most secret fantasies (the sodomy symbolised by the wheelbarrow). In his case we thus find referential elements such as the gold-painted wheel-barrow,

The Golden Goat of the Castle of Quermançó, *1979. Oil on wood, 234 × 140 cm.*

plates from Rosalyn Bacon's versions of Millet and eight copies of the first Spanish edition (1978) of *El mito tragico del Angelus de Millet (The Tragic Myth of the Angelus of Millet).*

We now come to a chamber which takes its name from the famous 1943 composition *Poetry of America.* This oil on canvas (116.8 × 78.7 cm) was painted in California during the Second World War. The period marked an important development in Dalí's attitude to the outside world, which he no longer tried to scorn (through the conquest of the irrational), but rather to master (using the magic of art). In this biographical context the "moralising" reading offered in *Poetry of America* takes on its full meaning: in a landscape (whose artificiality is underlined by the marble arch framing its upper section), two American footballer-rag dolls confront each other; the tower in the background (in a dream-like De Chirico vein) which oversees this fratricidal struggle displays the trophy of the skin of Africa bled dry of its original inhabitants, the slaves of America; the confrontation is not therefore sporting, but a racial fight to the death; a liquid pours from the right nipple of one of the players and is transformed into a bottle of Coca-Cola (the first appearance of the famous bottle in contemporary art), which itself turns into a receiver which dissolves into rotten ink; the excrescence of a small, new and hardly encouraging individual sprouts from the back of the other player.

Three further works complete the contents of this chamber: the chalk and lead pencil on paper monotype for the 1974 stereoscopy of the painter touching Gala's foot (60 × 62 cm); to the right and beside *Poetry of America*, there is another study in India ink, ball-point pen and sepia stains (150 × 102 cm) with angel figures; and next to the door we find a splendid 1940 lead pencil and *gouache* (77 × 56 cm) sketch of a chained maiden, a female centaur riding a small figure, and the central monstrous figure (whose left sandal is a veritable display of virtuoso skills).

Motif of the Escorial with Angels, *1970. India ink, ballpoint pen and sepia ink, 150 × 102 cm.*

Centaur, *1940. Lead pencil and gouache on paper, 77 × 56 cm.*

All along the corridor as far as the open arch on the first level over the stage we find a collection of lithographs belonging to two published works: *La vida es sueño* by Calderón, on which Dalí started work in 1962, and the 1964 *Mitologías*. The splendid 1968 lithograph (69 × 90 cm), with the image of a rhinoceros emerging from the roughness of a mossy stone (in a clear reference to the famous Dürer engraving in which the rhinoceros, according to Dalí, has a "lace suit" like those made by Vermeer's *Lacemaker*) deserves special attention.

In this corridor leading to the arch opening onto the stage we find two illustrative works on the subject of monotheism, including the splendid edition of the essay by Freud. Let us first study the wall at the end of the corridor, where Dalí placed an installation made up of symbolic elements linked by the theme of monotheism: the plaster reproduction 245 cm in height of Michaelangelo's *Moses*, over which we find a wooden sculpture with golden shapes of octopuses (the symbol of convergence, with a monotheistic head constituting a superior unity and the legs plurality) and a rhinoceros head (whose symbolic meaning consists in nature's renunciation of bipolarity in the perfect logarithmic morphology of the unicorn);

The Trial of Paris, *from the Mythologies series, 1964. Engraving, 75 × 55 cm.*

Poetry of America, *1943. Oil on canvas, 116 × 78.7 cm.*

and, respectively, to the left and right of *Moses*, the spectacular cases of the 1974 edition of Freud's *Moses and Monotheism* (79 × 55 cm) illustrated by Dalí, and the 1976 *L'Alchimie des Philosophes* (83 × 62 cm).

Once we have taken in the symbolic intention of this installation we can move on to the four lithographs on papyrus on the wall (65.5 × 52cm) from the edition just mentioned, complemented by the title page (on goat-skin), by four chapter pages of intaglio engravings and the plate illustration of *Moses's* head. This area also contains the untitled oil painting of the neo-classical statue of a woman split down the middle, with an egg at its centre and shot through with white arrows (whose deliberate location by Dalí in this monographic space constitutes something of a mystery).

To the left of the Moses installation we find the entrance to the Hall of Jewels, where Dalí displays his passion for goldsmithery, dating from the fifties on. Most of the jewellery on show here were produced in the seventies, in gold using cire-perdue casting, with occasional encrustations or

Christ of Limpias: *reproduction of Christ of the Agonies from the parish of Limpias (Cantabria), on paint and a sculptural* assemblage.

metallized paper additions. However, the first thing we come to in the hall is a large composition made up of the prototype for an articulated and mobile stained-glass cross by Pérez Piñero and the *The Cybernetic Princess* urn. Shortly before his death the architect of the latticed glass dome finished the prototype of the stained-glass cross, made up of 36 20 × 20 cm perspex plates which fold and unfold with the help of a mechanism whose enlarged reproduction was to be installed, like a theatre curtain, between the stage and the patio of the Teatre-Museu. These translucent plates were illuminated by Dalí with a variety of themes, around a central radial structure. Below the stained-glass cross we find a reproduction of the 160 cm. jade mummy, found together with a whole army of life-sized infantry and horsemen with individual features at the fabulous Ling-Tuong (Xian) archaeological site. By way of this 1974 reproduction Dalí establishes an association between the emblematic value and morphology of the mummy's jade plates and that of the printed circuits of contemporary computer science (which he used, once metallized and coloured, in the execution of the reproduction).

At the end of the hall, behind a protective glass screen, we come to the reproduction that the South American multimillionaire Arturo López had made of the inside of the Templete de Bramante in Rome. Dalí accepted the donation of the Templete in order to house his collection of small gold sculptures. Among these we should note the reproduction of the popular *Christ of the Agony* from the parish of Limpias in Cantabria (52 cm in height), with encrustations of quartz and a landscape of the Ampurdan, above the metallised skeleton of a fish and a small headless and armless nude in turn stepping on a fossil snail painted in black, and the two montages consisting of turtles being ridden by metallized paper figures (22 × 40 and 16 × 30 cm).

Argos, *from the* Mythologies *series, 1964. Lithograph, 56 × 75 cm.*

1974 reproduction, with printed circuit boards, of the jade sarcophagus found on the Ling-Tuong archaeological site.

THE TORRE GALATEA (THE HALL OF STEREOSCOPIES, LOGGIAS 1 AND 2, AND THE LAST ROOM OF THE VISIT).

Turning left we enter the Torre Galatea from the Hall of Jewels (the former Casa Gorgot, incorporated into the Teatre-Museu on 12 October 1983 and rebaptised *Galatea* by Dalí in memory of Gala, who died on June 10, 1982). This first space or *loggia* opens on the left onto the patio of the Torre Galatea (the corridor of Poetry of America mentioned above also opens onto it). With its benches, trees and small pond it is an ideal resting place during our visit. Visitors resting in the patio and gazing at the façade of the former theatre are unaware that this is the same view as Dalí had in the last years of his life from his bedroom in the Torre Galatea. Dalí loved looking at this wall which for him contained the whole universe; like a philosopher who had conquered wisdom he stated that he needed no more than this.

The visit to this first *loggia* begins with four "anamorphic" pieces next to the entrance door. They are four lithographs showing, respectively, a skull (73 × 55 cm), a horseman with a standard (54.6 × 74.5 cm), a female nude (86.2 × 61 cm) and a harlequin (86 × 61 cm), images which can only be seen in reflection in a cylindrical reflecting surface (a bottle of Ponche Caballero, to be precise). The old optical illusion of anamorphosis, which goes back to the seventeenth century, might be seen as just a display of technical skills on the part of Dalí. But we know by this stage of the visit that there is nothing gratuitous or "innocent" in Dalí: the fact of anamorphosis invites us to reflect on the psychological mechanisms of our reading of external reality, whose forms only acquire meaning through the (tautological) operation of granting them meaning (the mind acting like the bottle of Ponche Caballero and structured according to a system of cultural referents).

The spectacle of the hyper-realist stereoscopies we now come to has to do also with this reflection. In the seventies Dalí researched, first by painting classical stereoscopies, or doubles, then expanding them with the introduction of Wheatstone mirrors carried out by Roger de Montebello, later crossing images from different stereoscopies to produce a new image on the retina using Bela Julesz's anaglyphic structures. It is obvious that Dalí's primary intention is to offer us the virtual image of the third dimension (without which, according to him, the "experience of spirituality" cannot exist), carried to the limits of a feeling of infinity. The centre of each of the double paintings is always slightly "off", given the centimetres separating the spectator's eyes, and the copies are therefore never symmetrical; we should notice that the colours change, sometimes radically, from one stereoscopy to another, so that the colours finally perceived only exist on the retina and in the brain of the viewer. We are therefore once again confronted with the lived experience of a reality that does not exist (the final stereoscopical image), whose virtuality is the exclusive product of the magic of art.

Thus on the right-hand wall, so that visitors can fully grasp Dalí's intention here, a number of stereoscopical montages are usually on display in which the stereograms are photographic reproductions of the original oil paintings (with photographs by Robert Descharnes and Marc Lacroix). Next in the Hall of Stereoscopies we come to the original double oil paintings which cannot be viewed in a mirror installation due to lack of space. The paintings as they are exhibited thus lose the virtual relief effect, but on the other hand they do allow us to study their colours and details more closely.

To the right we see *Dalí with His Back Turned Painting Gala with Her Back Turned Eternalized in Six Virtual Corneas Provisionally Reflected in Six Real Mirrors* (double oil on canvas, 60 cm × 60 cm, 1972-1973), in one section of which the mirror image of the painter and his model is left unfinished. We know that this work was especially dear to Dalí, since there is a third version of it to be found among the treasures of his collection in the Hall of Masterpieces. We come next to *Dalí Raising a Golden Veil in the Shape of a Cloud to Show Gala the Naked Dawn Very Far Beyond the Sun. Homage to Claude Lorrain* (double oil on canvas, 205 × 138 cm, 1977). This large work is based on a Claude Lorrain (1600-1682) theme, into which Dalí introduces the impossible figure of the huge naked Auroras or dawn, while other traders go about their dealings unaware of the wonder.

In the right corner there is a small chamber (the inside of the base of the Torre Gorgot and the ancient fortifications of the city walls) which Dalí baptised *The Tower of All Enigmas*. Inside we find a small but highly theatrical masterpiece of stereoscopy (in a portable stereoscopic case): *The

*Torre Galatea, "gooseflesh"
façade with triangular loaves,
designed by Dalí in 1983.*

Hand of Dalí (double oil on canvas, 35 × 26.5 cm, c. 1972).
The contrast of colours between the stereograms is extreme
and there is a surprising formal difference in the length of
the forearm; the effect of depth and infinity (which Dalí re-
lates to the sensual experience of the spiritual) can be said
to be perfect. Here we also find the hologram *Holos! Holos!
Velazquez! Gabor!* (42 × 57 cm, c. 1972-73) on whose technical aspects the Hungarian physicist Dennis Gabor, the father of holography, worked together with Dalí. In this first
three-dimensional *collage* Dalí plays with the image of
astronauts drinking beer and the figure of Velazquez to
form the lower border of the dress of one of the infantas in
Las Meninas.
The facing wall is entirely given over to *The Chair*, a large
work (double oil on canvas, 401.5 × 211 cm, 1975). It should be
noted that the direction of Gala's gaze is marked out by a sort
of avenue of white washbasins (of the same make as those

Nude, *1972. Lithograph,*
86.8 × 61.6 cm.

crowning the upper level of the patio) and that in the left-hand oil painting Dalí's hand does not block the view of the small bottle resting on the first sink.

On the fourth wall we find the three last stereoscopies of the hall. The first is *Las Meninas* (double oil on canvas, 92 × 80 cm, 1975-76), a work in which Dalí insists on the baroque theme of the painter painting a picture viewed by the spectator, three dimensions of stereoscopic depth thus being superimposed, each one of which contains the next like a set of Chinese boxes or Russian dolls. Next we come to the stereoscopy entitled *Dalí Lifting the Skin of the Mediterranean Sea to Show Gala the Birth of Venus* (double oil on canvas, 101 × 101 cm, 1977). In this work Dalí combines a treatment similar to that used for the huge naked body of the homage to Claude Lorrain with the iconography of some representative fifties oil paintings, in which the calm surface of the sea is shown as a skin on which can support the girl-boy Dalí's weight or allow him to lift it. The last stereoscopy in the hall is *Gala's Foot* (double oil on canvas, 60 cm × 60 cm, 1974), in which the theme of the painting within the painting

Harlequin, *1972. Lithograph, 87 × 61.9 cm.*

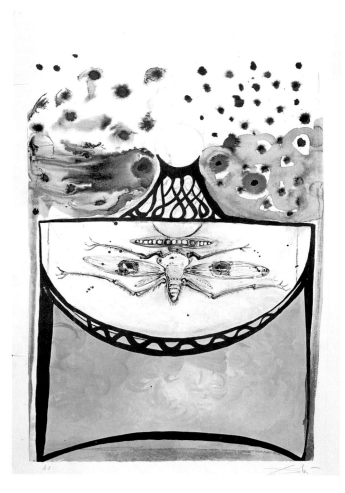

is presented in the form of a stereoscopy within a stereoscopy (since the picture on Dalí's easel is one of the stereograms with his vision of DNA which we have already seen here); Gala's smiles are worth noting (one of them is almost a caricature).

The exit from the Hall of Stereoscopies allows access to the second *loggia* of the Torre Galatea, where we find on the right a poster for the bullfight which took place in Figueres on 12 August 1961, as one of the events promoting the Teatre-Museu. The sketch *Helicopter and Bull* has been attached to the poster in *collage* fashion. (Let us recall that, according to Dalí's plans, the carcass of this totemic animal was to be removed vertically from the bullring by helicopter and dropped onto the Wagnerian peaks of Montserrat.)

The next piece is an extremely significant 1974 work entitled *Dalí Writing His Tragedy* (smoke and gouache on paper, 153 × 103 cm), since Dalí here portrays himself in his old age with a skull and a book in which is he is writing (in indescribable "catastrophist" handwriting) the lonely trag-

Gala's Foot, 1974. Double oil on canvas, each stereoscopical panel 60 × 60 cm.

edy of his life as a "genius", as a thin arm is raised in admonition, as if warning him to finish his legacy for posterity before it is too late.

The last space we are going to visit was original dedicated in its entirety to Francesc Pujols, whose baroque thought and intuition always awakened Dalí's interest and respect. On the wall facing the entrance we thus find a homage to Pujols made of a large anonymous still life of the Flemish School which Dalí altered during the time he spent in Port Lligat in 1972-73. This oil painting, entitled *"Cuant cau, cau"* (sic), in other words, *When It Falls, It Falls* (196 × 297.5 cm), the literal quotation of a tautological aphorism. Dalí adds surrealistic baroque touches to the already baroque elements from the original still life, as a homage to the delirious and dense prose of Pujols. What is it, though, that falls "fatally' under its own weight in the images of this picture? Dalí seems to be illustrating the very process of the decomposition of matter, not without a tragic sense of humour: the soft

(and edible) matter that transforms the figure of the pictures and converts the culinary elements of the picture into a lucid and foreboding nightmare of the physical disasters of death.

The remaining walls of the hall contain works from the artist's last period. To the right and left of the entrance we find two oils on canvas from the series *The Enigmas of Gala*, which include the horizontal profile of the Aphrodite of Cnidus, in grey and ochres of striking delicacy; in the left-hand painting, simply entitled *Enigma* (100 × 99.8 cm), the profile appears once, while in *The Three Enigmas of Gala* (100 x100 cm), to the right, the profile is repeated three times, accompanied by seated figures representing youth and old age. On the right-hand wall we find another two oils on canvas referring to Velazquez ("Velazquez tells me more about light than tons of scientific tracts. He is an inexhaustible treasure of exact calculi and data"). *The Pearl, after "La Infanta Margarita"* (140 × 100 cm, 1981) is located to the

Dalí Lifting the Skin of the Mediterranean Sea to Show Gala the Birth of Venus, *1977. Double oil on canvas, each stereoscopical panel 101 × 101 cm.*

right and *After "The Landlord José Nieto"* (140 × 100 cm, 1982) to the left of the same wall. All through this series there is an underlying identification with the loneliness of the genius of Seville, incarnated in *Velazquez Dying By the Window, to the Left, Where a Spoon Appears* (oil on canvas with *collages*, 75 × 59.5 cm) in the horrifying gaze of Sebastian de Morra — one of the jester-dwarves of the palace — which has seen everything and expects nothing. The mentioned works show what might be termed an astronomical interpretation of the position of the figures in *Las Meninas:* from his window, opening onto the Sierra de Guadarrama, Velazquez saw the Corona Borealis constellation, whose pattern of stars coincides literally with the position of the heads of the seven figures of *Las Meninas*. This reading is even more obvious in the head of the Infanta Margarita (the "pearl" of the constellation). The traced squares on this second oil painting therefore do not indicate that it is unfinished, since according to Dalí they had a similar function,

whatever it might be, to the white diagonal form in the former.

Two further 1981 oils on canvas are on display on the left-hand wall of this room: *Mercury and Argos* (140 × 95 cm, 1981), and *The Apparition of the Face of the Aphrodite of Cnidus in a Landscape* (140 × 95 cm, 1981). Whatever about the mythological content of this first painting, what is most striking is the terrifying gaze of the eyes of the main figure, which seem have seen the horror of horrors. In the second painting, however, the treatment of the face recalls the serene lyricism of the series *The Enigmas of Gala*, this time in the face of Aphrodite in the shape of a tombstone which extends into the a dreamlike infinity.

As we leave this room through the doorway of the *loggia* we come to, on the right, the final painting of our visit (at least until the Theatre-Museum is expanded further), the *Figure of an Angel* (wash, sanguine and gouache on card-

Cuant, cau, cau [sic] (Homage to
Pujols), *1972-73. 196 × 297 cm.
Painted onto a Flemish still life.*

board, 152.2 × 192 cm, 1970). Perhaps no other figure could
provide a more fitting end for our visit to the Theatre of
Dalinian Memory than this Angel of Death which raises its
tunic to show us its carnal and splendid backside by way of
farewell.

CODA: DALI'S BEQUEST AND "THE APOTHEO-SIS OF THE DOLLAR".

It is well known that Dalí left
the works contained in his collection to the Spanish State;
as a result of the series of conversation initiated by the
then Minister of Culture, the writer Jorge Semprún, a rea-
sonable agreement was reached whereby the collection was
split between the Centro de Arte Reina Sofía in Madrid and
the Teatre-Museu Dalí in Figueres. The Teatre-Museu has
in its possession more than a hundred works from this divi-
sion of Dalí's bequest to be hung in its new spaces or to
alternate with the pictures contained in some of the halls. It
should be observed, finally, that the periods best represented in this bequest are the twenties (14 works), the sixties
(13 works), the seventies (28 works) and the eighties (63
works). One of the most representative works of the mature
Dalí (on show in the new extension of the museum adjoining
the Torre Galatea, in the Pujada de la Creu) is present
thanks to the acquisition policy of the Fundació Gala-Salvador Dalí. *Dalí in the Process of Painting Gala in the Apotheosis of the Dollar; in Which Marcel Duchamp Can Also
Be Seen to the Left Disguised as Louis XIV, Behind a Ver-
meer-Style Curtain Which Is None Other Than the Invisible But Monumental Face of Hermes* (oil on Canvas, 400 ×

The Pearl, after "The Infanta
Margarita", *1981. Oil on canvas,
140 × 100 cm.*

498 cm, 1965), a work always known as *The Apotheosis of the Dollar*.

The outlandish title of this work, with its chain of allusion to the double, triple and multiple images contained in this oil painting — excessive in every sense of the word — points towards the fact that the only unacceptable reading would be one simply glorifying money. (We already know what Dalí thinks of the false and paralysing value of gold.) Interpreting this piece is, nonetheless, a complex process giving rise to all sorts of hypotheses; but everything seems to indicate that we are dealing with alchemical gold whose "apotheosis" is manifested in the work of art. In other words, the power of the work of art is the only power capable of transforming the dollar, in a sort of apotheosis, into art, and not the other way around. We are, in any case, definitely dealing with a paranoiac-critical delirium involving double images in which Dalí, at the age of sixty-one, seems to be offering us an autobiographical compendium of his intellectual and aesthetic obsessions, harmonising them in a visual labyrinth in which the attentive viewer can slowly discover an infinity of visual

Portrait of René Crevel, *1934.*
India ink and gouache on paper,
72 × 63 cm.

Apparition of the Face of the
Aphrodite of Cnidus in a
Landscape, *1981. Oil on canvas,*
1981, 140 × 95 cm.

puns, paranoiac-critical associations: Hermes, Vermeer, Duchamp, Ceres, Mercury, Bernini, Molière, Fortuny, Napoleon, Meissonier, Llull, Quevedo, Velazquez, Dalí and Gala, among others.

The Foundation has also announced the acquisition of other works at present on show in its new spaces: the representative *Inaugural Gooseflesh* (whose shape is extremely characteristic of an multiplication sign or spinning top). This 1928 oil painting on wood (75.5 × 62.5 cm) was originally entitled *Surrealistic Composition* and is comparable in terms of content and technique to such central works as *Cinderella* and *Honey Is Sweeter Than Blood*. The second acquisition is the *Portrait of René Crevel* (India ink and gouache, 72 × 63 cm), 1934, one of two portraits which are evidence of the excellent friendship of Gala and Dalí with the writer when they were fellow militants in the ranks of Breton's surrealism. It is strange that both portraits contain symbols of death, for they anticipated the suicide of the writer by a few months.

Lastly, and by way of a final comment, we hope that our fellow-traveller the visitor will share our confidence that time is working with rather than against a growing understanding and appreciation of the (tragic) phenomenological reflections and the work, both literary and graphic, of Salvador Dalí —

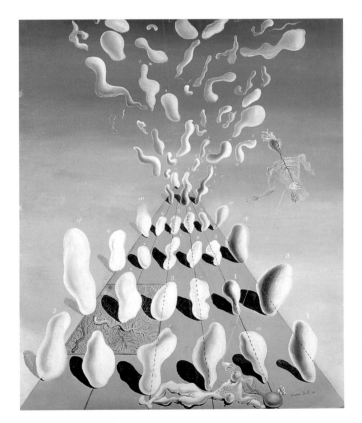

Inaugural Gooseflesh, *1928. Oil on canvas, 75.5 × 62.5 cm.*

the son of the notary of Figueres who wanted to be a painter, and who, while playing at being a genius from childhood on, came to be one of the greatest and most misunderstood geniuses of the century.

"The Apotheosis of the Dollar", *1965. Oil on canvas, 400 × 498 cm.*

Bibliography

Ades, Dawn, *Salvador Dalí*, Folio, Barcelona, 1984.

Barey, André, "La *Posició moral del Surrealismo* by Salvador Dalí", in *L'Avenç*, no. 84, Barcelona, 1985.

Brihuega, Jaime, *Miró y Dalí: los grandes surrealistas*, Anaya, Madrid, 1993.

Cabañas Bravo, MIguel, "El joven Dalí entre la tradición y la vanguardia artística", in *Archivo Español de Arte*, no. 250, Madrid, 1990

Clara, Josep, "Salvador Dalí, empresonat per la dictadura de Primo de Rivera", in *Revista de Girona*, no. 162, Girona, 1994.

Cowles, Fleur, *El caso Salvador Dalí*, Noguer, Barcelona, 1959.

Crevel, René, *Dalí o el antioscurantismo*, Olañeta Editor, Barcelona-Palma, 1978.

Dalí, Anna M. *Noves imatges de Salvador Dalí*, Columna, Barcelona, 1988.

Dalí, Salvador (selection):
— "Poema de les cosetes", in *L'Amic de les Arts*, no. 27, Sitges, 1928.
— "Un chien andalou" (script with Luis Buñuel), a *La revue du cinéma*, no. 5, Paris, 1929.
— *La femme visible*, Éditions Surréalistes, Paris, 1930.
— *L'amour et la mémoire*. Éditions Surréalistes, Paris, 1931.
— *Babaouo*, Cahiers Libres, Paris, 1932. *Babaouo*, Labor, Barcelona, 1978.
— "De la beauté terrifante et comestible de l'architecture Modern Style", in *Minotaure*, no. 3-4-, Paris, 1933.
— *La conquête de l'irrationnel*, Éditions Surréalistes, Paris, 1935.
— *Métamorphose du Narcisse*, Éditions Surréalistes, Paris, 1937.
— *The Secret Life of Salvador Dalí*, Dial Press. New York, 1942. *Vida secreta de Salvador Dalí*, DASA, Figueres, 1981.
— *Hidden Faces*, Dial Press, New York, 1944. *Rostros ocultos*, Luis de Caralt, Barcelona, 1952; Plaza Janés, Barcelona, 1984.

— *Fifty Secrets of Magic Craftmanship*. Dial Press. New York, 1948. *Cincuenta secretos mágicos para pintar*, Luis de Caralt, Barcelona, 1951.
— *Manifeste mystique*, R. J. Godet, París, 1951.
— *Les cocus du vieil art moderne*, Flasquelle, Paris, 1956. *Los cornudos del viejo arte moderno*, Tusquets, Barcelona, 1990.
— *Le mythe tragique de l'Angelus de Millet, interprétation paranoïque-critique*, Pauvert, Paris, 1963. *El mito trágico del "Ángelus" de Millet*, Tusquets, Barcelona, 1978.
— *Journal d'un génie*, La Table Ronde, Paris, 1964. *Diario de un genio*, Tusquets, Barcelona, 1983.
— *Oui*, Denoël, Paris, 1971. *Sí*, Ariel, Barcelona, 1977.
— *Dix recettes d'immortalité*, Audouin-Descharnes, Paris, 1973.
— *Cenas de Gala*, Labor, Barcelona, 1973.
— *Carta abierta a Salvador Dalí*, Ultramar Editores, Madrid, 1976.
— *Confesiones inconfesables*, Planeta, Barcelona, 1977.

Dalí, Salvador; Gasch, Sebastià i Montanyà, Lluís, *Manifest Groc* (facsimile of the edition by F. Sabater, Barcelona, 1928), Leteradura, Barcelona, 1977.

Dalí, Salvador i Pla, Josep, *Obres de Museu*, DASA, 1981.

Descharnes, Robert, *Dalí de Gala*, Lazarus, Lausanne, 1962.
— *Dalí. La obra y el hombre*. Tusquets Editor, Barcelona, 1984.
— *Dalí*, Harry N. Abrams, New York, 1985.
— *La vie de Salvador Dalí*, Paris, 1986.

Descharnes, Robert i Néret, Gilles, *Salvador Dalí*, Sheisha, Tokyo, 1974.

Various authors
Fanés, Fèlix. (ed.), *Dalí escriptor*, Fundació Caixa de Pensions, Barcelona, 1990.
— "Dalí reivindica Gaudí", in *Nexus*, no. 11. Fundació Caixa de Catalunya, Barcelona, 1993.

Fornés, Eduard, *Dalí i els llibres*, Mediterrània, Barcelona, 1982.

Gérard, Max i Dr. Roumeguère, P, *Dalí... Dalí... Dalí...*, Galaxis, Barcelona, 1974.

Giménez-Frontín, José Luis, *El surrealismo*, Dopesa, Barcelona, 1978.

— "Una carta a Juan Ramón Jiménez, medio siglo después", in *Estudios sobre Juan Ramón Jiménez*, Recinto Universitario de Mayagüez, Puerto Rico, 1981.

Gómez de la Serna. Ramón, *Dalí*, Espasa Calpe, Madrid, 1976.

Gómez de Liaño, Ignacio, *Dalí*, La Poligrafa, Barcelona, 1982.

— "Dalí", in *Mi tiempo*, Ediciones Libertarias, Madrid, 1984.

Guardiola Rovira, Ramón, *Dalí y su Museo. La obra que no quiso Bellas Artes*. Editoria Ampordanesa, Figueres, 1984.

— *Dalí de primera mà*, Gironina, Girona 1990.

Lear, Amanda, *L'amant Dalí*, Lafont, Paris, 1994.

Llarch, Juan, *Biografía mágica*, Plaza Janés, Barcelona, 1983.

Lopsinger, Lutz W. i Michler, Ray, *Catalogue raisoné of etchings and mixed-media prints, 1924-1980*, Prestel, 1994.

Masolliver, Juan Ramón, "Possibilitats i hipocresia del surrealisme d'Espanya", in *Butlletí de l'Agrupament Escolar*, no. 7-9, Barcelona, 1930.

Maur, Karin von, "Breton et Dalí, à la lumière d'une correspondance inédite", in *André Breton. La beauté convulsive*, Centre Georges Pompidou, Paris, 1991.

Minguet Batllori, Joan M (ed.), *Salvador Dalí i el cinema*, Filmoteca de la Generalitat de Catalunya, Barcelona, 1991.

— "El cinema(fo)tógrafo dalinianc", in *Archivos. Revista de estudios históricos sobre la imagen*, núm. 8, Valencia, 1991.

Molas, Joaquim, "Salvador Dalí, entre el surrealisme i el marxisme". in *L'Avenç*, no. 32, Barcelona, 1980.

— *La literatura catalana d'avantguarda (1916-1938)*, Antoni Bosch, Barcelona, 1983.

Morse, A. Reynolds, *Salvador Dalí. A Collection*, The Salvador Dalí Museum, Cleveland, 1972.

— *Salvador Dalí. A Guide to his Work in Public Museums*, The Salvador Dalí Museum, Cleveland, 1974.

— *Salvador Dalí. Ninety-three Oils*, 1917-1970, The Salvador Dalí Museum, Cleveland, 1974.

Orwell, George, "Benefit of Clergy. Some Notes on Salvador Dalí", in *Decline of the English Murder*, Penguin, Harmondsworth, 1965.

Parinaud, A, *Confesiones inconfesables*, Bruguera, Barcelona, 1975.

Pas, Annemieke van de, *Salvador Dalí. L'obra literària*, Mediterrània, Barcelona, 1989.

Pla, Josep, *Tres artistes catalanes: Dalí, Gaudí, Nonell*, Alianza, Madrid, 1986.

Puig, Arnau, "Salvador Dalí surrealista", in *Escrits d'Estètica. Filosofies*, Laertes, Barcelona, 1987.

Ramírez, Juan A, "Dalí: lo crudo y lo podrido. El cuerpo desgarrado y la matanza", in *La Balsa de la Medusa*, no. 12, 1989.

Rodrigo, Antonina, *Lorca-Dalí, una amistad traicionada*, Planeta, Barcelona, 1981.

Rodríguez Aguilera, Cesáreo, *Dalí*, Ediciones Nauta, Barcelona, 1985.

Rojas, Carlos, *El mundo mítico y mágico de Salvador Dalí*, Plaza Janés, Barcelona, 1985.

Romero, Luis, *Todo Dalí en un rostro*, Blume, Barcelona, 1975.

— *Dedálico Dalí*, Ediciones B, Barcelona, 1989.

— *PsicoDALÍco DALÍ*, Mediterrània, Barcelona, 1991.

— *Salvador Dalí*, Edicions. 62, Barcelona, 1992.

Sánchez Vidal, Agustín, *Buñuel, Lorca, Dalí*, Planeta, Barcelona, 1988.

Santos Torroella, Rafael, *La miel es más dulce que la sangre. Las épocas lorquiana y freudiana de Salvador Dalí*, Seix Barral, Barcelona, 1984.

— *Salvador Dalí i el Saló de Tardor. Un episodi de la vida artística barcelonina el 1928*, Reial Acadèmia de Belles Arts de Sant Jordi, Barcelona, 1985.

— *Salvador Dalí corresponsal de J.V. Foix, 1932-1936*, Mediterrània, Barcelona, 1986.

— "Salvador Dalí escribe a Federico García Lorca (1925-1936)", in *Poesía*, no. 27-28, Madrid, 1987.

Shanes, E, *Dalí*, Debate, Madrid, 1992.

Smith, Meredith Etherington, *The persistente of memory*, Random, Nova York, 1993.

Tharrats, Joan-Josep, *Surrealisme a l'Empordà*, Parsifal, Barcelona, 1993.

Diversos autores, *Salvador Dalí. Rétrospective, 1920-1980*, Paris, 1979.

— *Dalí*, The Stratton Foundation, Milano, 1989.

— *Dalí i els llibres*, Generalitat de Catalunya, Barcelona, 1982.

— *400 obres de Salvador Dalí del 1914 al 1983*, Generalitat de Catalunya, Ministerio de Cultura, Caixa de Pensions, Barcelona, 1983.

— *Salvador Dalí, 1904-1989*, Staatsgalerie, Stuttgart, 1989.

— *Homenatge a Salvador Dalí i Domènech, Marquès de Pùbol*, Fundació Gala-Salvador Dalí, Figueres, 1990.

— *The Salvador Dalí Museum Collection*, Bulfinch Press, Boston-Toronto-London, 1991.

— *Las vanguardias en Cataluña (1906-1939)* i *Avantguardes a Catalunya (1906-1939)*, Fundació Caixa de Catalunya, Barcelona, 1992.

— *Dalí-El Pan*, Tusquets Editor, Barcelona, 1903.

— *Salvador Dalí. The Early Years*, South Bank Centre, London, 1994.